The Dummies Guide to Start Your Own Business

Table Of Contents:

Introduction

Starting and running a business is often seen as a rewarding way to earn a living, despite the challenges it involves. To be a successful entrepreneur, you need more than just hard work and commitment. You also need specific personality traits and business habits that are usually found among successful people in this field. These traits are crucial in shaping the choices entrepreneurs make an impact the fundamental principles and daily operations of their businesses.

Whether you're considering starting a new business or looking for ways to improve an existing one, this book will offer invaluable advice and guidance. By following the strategies outlined in this book, you can significantly boost your chances of starting a profitable business or rejuvenating your current one.

Running a business isn't always easy, but with the right mindset and a well-thought-out strategy, you can set yourself up for success. This involves carefully evaluating your needs, creating a robust business plan, and completing all the necessary legal paperwork before you start. Once you have a sound business strategy and the financial resources needed to reach your goals, you'll be well on your way to launching a successful and prosperous venture.

In the following sections of this book, we'll explore the specific expectations every business owner must meet to successfully establish, manage, and grow their business or firm, both offline and online. Whether you're exploring traditional physical business models or stepping into the digital world, we'll provide you with the essential knowledge and tools to confidently and expertly navigate each area.

Throughout this comprehensive guide, we'll cover important topics such as cultivating a winning mindset, conducting market research, creating compelling branding, implementing effective marketing strategies, managing finances, building outstanding teams, and growing your business for long-term success.

By diving into these valuable insights, you'll gain a deep understanding of what it takes to succeed as an entrepreneur in today's fast-paced business environment.

Remember, and I can't stress this enough: building and managing a successful business requires constant learning, adaptation, and commitment.

This book aims to equip you with the knowledge and resources to overcome challenges, seize opportunities, and build a business that not only survives but thrives. So, prepare yourself for an enlightening journey that will enable you to realize your entrepreneurial dreams and take your business to unprecedented levels of success.

Chapter 1: The one thing you need to succeed in business

If you have a unique skill that others lack, you might have what it takes to establish a business. Sometimes, all it takes is the readiness to offer something that others can't or won't.

There are various reasons and methods to initiate a business. Perhaps you're looking to diversify the revenue streams of an existing business, or maybe you're aiming to boost your income or gain more control over your life.

Many people believe that there's a single leap between their current situation and their desired outcome. However, reaching any goal is more like climbing a staircase. If your first step is to follow the guidance in this book, your chances of success will significantly increase.

Your task is to identify and understand all the necessary steps to practically achieve your goal, tailored to your specific startup. It might be tempting to skip a step or two to get to the exciting parts faster. But rest assured, if you follow and complete each step, starting with the first one, your ascent will be more stable.

Conversely, taking the wrong initial step could lead you to miss your goal entirely.

When should you start a business?

A common question many people ask is about the ideal time to start a business. The best response to this is akin to the answer to the question: When is the best time to plant a tree? Twenty years ago.

Some people wait as if they're expecting a divine sign. Others wait for a significant event to signal the start, like the firing of a starting gun. Some wait until they're in a desperate situation with nothing left to lose, having already lost so much. It's advisable not to wait that long.

If something significant does occur, that's great, use it. But often, something meaningful happens when you simply start, and your startup might just succeed.

The aim of this book is to motivate you to start sooner rather than later. Even if you fail, you'll gain valuable lessons from the experience.

What is your business?

Broadly speaking, businesses can be classified as either service-based or product-based entities. They cover a wide range of industries, from agriculture to zoology and everything in between.

Choosing your business niche should always be influenced by your personal interests. If you don't enjoy your business, you're more likely to give up out of frustration or boredom when faced with challenges. Your passion for your industry will be the driving force that propels you to keep going, even during difficult times.

The Link Between Passion and Business

Your fervor for your business can act as a magnet, attracting potential clients, partners, vendors, and team members. However, it's crucial to remember that transforming your enthusiasm into a business venture comes with its own set of risks. The business environment is ever-changing, and your initial focus may shift over time. For instance, you may start with a love for cooking and professional culinary expertise, but your business might evolve to encompass more than just culinary arts.

The Art of Business and Customer Satisfaction

The key to being a prosperous business owner lies in ensuring customer satisfaction. Using the cooking analogy, the fundamental expectation of customers is the quality of the food you prepare. To retain them and earn their recommendations, you need to exceed their expectations, foster personal relationships with them, and establish proactive strategies to encourage their return.

The Risks and Disruptions of Outsourcing

Outsourcing tasks like customer acquisition and management might seem like a beneficial strategy, but it carries inherent risks. If a critical function that you've outsourced goes awry, it could negatively impact your business. Therefore, it's crucial to have a well-managed system or process in place for key tasks such as customer acquisition and retention.

The Cornerstones of Business: Quality and Sales

No matter what kind of business you operate, the pillars of success remain the same: efficient customer acquisition and management, quality assurance, and superior product or service. Even the most skilled salesperson cannot make up for a subpar product or service. This emphasizes the need for a knowledgeable sales team that understands not only the product but also the client's needs.

Learning from Sales Missteps

Sales can be a tricky field, particularly if there is a lack of understanding about the services or the clients. A personal experience of losing a client due to a sales representative's misinterpretation highlights the significance of this knowledge. It further stresses the need for technical experts, like chefs in the food industry, to participate in managing customer expectations and needs.

The Significance of Operational Systems

For your business to grow, it's essential to have operational systems in place across all sectors, including production, quality control, security, human resources, and training. These systems should be flexible to cater to a variety of customer needs. After all, the key to business success lies in fulfilling customer expectations, even if it means deviating from your initial plans.

Adjusting to Customer Preferences

It's vital for your business to adapt according to the needs of your customers. For instance, if you are a pastry chef specializing in pastries but your customers are asking for different types of meals, you should consider modifying your offerings to meet their demands. This adaptability is crucial for the survival and profitability of your business.

The Experimental Aspect of Business

Operating a business can often feel like conducting an experiment. You may find that customers are attracted to your primary services and recommend you to others based on their positive experiences. However, these new customers might have their own preconceptions about what you offer. In such situations, it's important to clearly communicate your services, much like a chef's menu informs customers about the available dishes.

If you're uncertain about what kind of business to start, there are resources available, such as the book "Discovered, 505 Odd Enterprises" by George Haylings, which can provide you with numerous ideas. The main point to remember is to ensure your business aligns with customer demand.

Business Operations: The Foundation of Your Business

Streamlined business operations are crucial when it comes to managing a business. These operations, which span across sales, production, delivery, and finance, ensure the smooth functioning of your business. And at the core of these operations are your customers.

Comprehending and Satisfying Customer Needs

Understanding your customers' needs and figuring out how to meet them effectively is fundamental to your business. In fact, your primary objective should be to secure your first paying customer. This might involve offering a simple product or service in exchange for payment. In many instances, this could be a consultation service, which could be an effective way to launch your business.

The Reality of Business Failure

Regrettably, a large number of new businesses don't survive past their initial years. This is primarily due to the absence of a business plan, cash flow issues, or a lack of understanding of business fundamentals. These problems highlight the need to recognize that a business only truly exists when it has paying customers. Your job is to identify those people who are likely to become your customers. Often, the reasons why your customers make purchases are different from what you initially thought would attract them. Let's take a restaurant as an example. You might choose to open a pizza restaurant. Customers may not come for the pizza itself, but for the quiet, romantic, or private corners and atmosphere where they can enjoy the dining experience more than the food itself.

Finding Your First Paying Customer

To attract your first paying customer, think about offering a simple product or service. An advisory service could be a good starting point, where you get paid to train, consult, or explain how to perform a task. Your expertise is your greatest asset in this scenario.

How will you achieve success?

The key to business success is having a robust business plan, efficient operations, and a thorough understanding of business principles. However, remember that despite all your planning, customers often have different expectations, and your business needs to be flexible enough to adapt to customer needs. This implies that your business plan should act as a roadmap to get you started and keep you on track, but you should be ready to modify it to meet the demands of your paying customers. Most importantly, remember that your business exists to serve your customers. Therefore, your main goal is to understand their needs, exceed their expectations, and establish long-lasting relationships with them. And remember, anyone could potentially be a customer. So, go out there and find them.

Rethinking the Route to Your First Customer

Many people believe that a product or service must be completely developed before acquiring the first customer, which often leads to a self-perpetuating cycle of failure. This perspective can be flawed. Some business models require significant capital to start, and these are not considered in this book. Starting a business that requires a large investment when you have limited resources is a tough task. While borrowing may be an option, it often comes with conditions that leave you as an employee or partner rather than the owner. This book is not intended for those in such a situation.

Debt-free Business and Customer as a Capital Source

This book is aimed at those with limited investment resources and a reluctance to incur debt. The drawbacks of debt in business are numerous; if the business struggles, stagnates, or stops entirely, repaying the debt becomes a daunting task. The suggested approach here is to identify a customer, make a sale, and secure payment. In this way, your customer becomes your source of working capital, saving you from debt and helping you build capital. While this may seem overly simplistic, it's a strategy with significant value and has been the foundation for many successful businesses.

Understanding Your Customer

A customer is someone seeking a solution to a problem they're facing. Your role is to demonstrate that you can solve this problem and charge for your services. This is a fundamental business principle. Many potential customers are ready to address their issues and are often willing to pay in advance, especially in the online world.

Targeting Potential Customers

To identify potential customers, you need to understand who they are, and just as crucially, who they aren't. By eliminating certain market segments, you can concentrate your efforts, save time, and increase your chances of acquiring paying customers.

Preventing Cash Flow Issues

Cash flow problems are typically the most serious concern for startups. The allure of resorting to credit cards or bank loans can be strong, but this can create more problems than it resolves. These funds can quickly deplete and require repayment. The optimal cash flow strategy is to avoid spending money you don't have. The most effective way to prevent cash flow issues is to secure paying customers. It's advisable to establish a policy of requesting payment before, during, or after delivering your service or product.

Applying Theory to Practice

The advice given here isn't purely theoretical. I'm not a reporter or journalist; I'm sharing from my personal experience. In my business endeavors, I've found that being transparent about your startup status and asking for payment for problem-solving is an effective approach. The pricing should have been agreed upon beforehand; the discussion at this point is about when the payment will be made.

Gaining Confidence from Your First Customer

Acquiring your first customer can be a transformative experience. It's a clear indicator of success and prosperity. Envisioning this scenario can help you prepare for objections and negativity and build the confidence needed to secure your first customer. This isn't just an imaginative exercise but a way to adopt a success-oriented mindset. However, imagination alone isn't a solution; you still need to persuade a customer to purchase your product or service.

The Real Reward of Your First Customer

The benefit of securing your first customer extends beyond financial gain. While money is certainly important, the greater reward is the sense of pride and confidence boost you'll receive. This accomplishment serves as proof that your objectives are achievable, and it equips you with the knowledge to replicate the process.

The Safety of Starting a Business Without Money

Starting a business without an initial investment is arguably the safest way to enter entrepreneurship, as it creates a situation where you stand only to gain. The primary goal of a business is to generate income. If you invest your own money, especially at the beginning, you risk losing it. Therefore, acquiring customers first isn't just a cost-saving strategy; it's also about risk reduction.

Timing Investments and Growth Strategy

Investments should be made when your business is generating a consistent cash flow. The profits from your business should be the funds used for its growth. However, expansion should only occur once you've confirmed the viability of your business and feel comfortable moving forward with it.

Realizing That Practice Makes Perfect

Your first business venture doesn't have to be flawless. Perfection is achieved through practice, a universally accepted truth. Some people invest in businesses that align with their dreams, only to realize that the reality isn't as gratifying as they had imagined. For instance, during the lockdown, city dwellers heavily invested in rural farms, dreaming of a pastoral lifestyle. Many quickly realized that farm life wasn't for them and yearned to return to the city.

Equipping Yourself with Business Skills

The purpose of this book is to provide you with the necessary skills to ensure your business thrives. If you ever find yourself needing more money, these skills will lead you back to your customer base, your source of income. By learning how to fish, you can always return to the water for sustenance. This concept is at the heart of the philosophy of starting a business without any money.

Establish your enterprise on firm ground

When initiating a start-up or a new business, there are crucial factors to consider.

Throughout my career, I've collaborated with numerous entrepreneurs worldwide across various sectors. I've been privy to their aspirations and, in many instances, their triumphs. I've observed that the successful ones are truly committed to their craft and invest time in contemplating every facet of their business.

However, the distinction between success and failure boils down to those who prioritize customer needs and those who don't.

Prioritizing customers first implies that you're not concentrating on expenditures such as equipment, leases, capital investments, staff recruitment, location security, and so on.

Before the pandemic, one of the most common family investments was in restaurants. Families would pool resources to lease or purchase a location, then equip it with the latest kitchen gear. This process is time-consuming and often undertaken without understanding the customer's desires.

Interestingly, auctions are a great place to find affordable kitchen equipment, primarily because most restaurants fail.

Initiating your business

I often hear people prioritizing fundraising.

Or, they stumble upon an idea, believe they need to establish authority, and decide to get certified. If you can acquire a certification, by all means, do so. If you can raise funds, that's excellent. Just bear in mind that you must prioritize customer needs.

The first step is to identify a customer

I recommend finding someone who requires your services and assisting them.

If you're a chef, prepare delicious food and find a customer willing to pay for a chef's services. Do you really need a lavish restaurant before securing your first customer?

While location and atmosphere can contribute, remember that leasing or property purchase isn't necessary. Some customers will pay for a chef to come to their location. Many people pay for cooking lessons from a chef. When starting, consider quick and low-cost options. What can you do at little or no cost to generate income?

You can offer your services to potential customers at a discounted rate. Essentially, the quickest way to start a business is simply to begin. Above all, you need to assist customers who know what they want. You only assume you know what they want.

Initial business ideas rarely match the final business model. All businesses evolve to cater to customer needs. Anticipate changes from the outset. Consider what you can modify so potential customers perceive you as adaptable, unique, and a likely better match.

For instance, several successful 'flying' chefs cook exquisite meals in your kitchen, at your home. This is particularly popular for hosting events, where the chef becomes the evening's star attraction.

The second step is to be transparent with your customer

Be truthful, inform your potential customers about the deal, explain why you want to assist them, and clarify how you can and cannot help.

If they still want to collaborate with you after all that, fantastic.

Avoid guaranteeing success if you're unsure about your customers' definition of success. The key is not to make commitments you can't fulfill. If possible, under-promise and over-deliver. Over-delivering will enhance your reputation and attract business through referrals. In the early stages, you need as many case studies as possible to prove and demonstrate your capabilities to others.

The third key is to establish your conditions

This is a crucial aspect of being transparent with your client, especially when it comes to the financial aspect. If you intend to charge for your services, you need to make this clear from the start. Many people seek assistance, but you want clients who are willing to pay. There are different methods to approach this. You might need to cover expenses, require a deposit, or simply state that although you're happy to help, your service and time need to be prepaid.

You have the flexibility to set a fixed price for the entire job or an hourly or daily rate. You can also establish a minimum or maximum in terms of hours or pay rate. It's your decision or something you can negotiate.

When you strike a deal with a potential client, they understand that payment is necessary at some point. If an upfront payment is required, don't start the job until they've agreed to pay you in advance.

It's always wise to have your client's agreement in writing. For instance, in a restaurant, prices and menu items are clearly displayed so customers know what they're paying for in advance.

Don't hesitate to ask for the order to proceed. In a restaurant, orders are usually taken by a waiter and confirmed before being sent to the kitchen. In other businesses, you might have a conversation and then confirm via email what you've agreed upon. This is the foundation on which you'll carry out the work.

As your business grows, you'll have terms and conditions posted on your website. You'll draft contracts for clients to sign and request purchase orders. These are standard practices for established businesses, and you can adopt them too if you wish.

These three key steps are crucial when starting a business. Going through them might prompt you to refine your ideas and processes. Keep in mind that most clients want you to tailor your services to their needs.

Avoid providing free service

Providing services to a potential client for free can be unwise and costly.

Offering a free trial is often considered an option, and first-time authors frequently give away their books for free. However, be aware that you might attract the wrong type of client, one who never intends to pay. Moreover, if there's no charge, there might not be a clear order. Without a clear order, there's likely no clear understanding of what's expected, making it impossible for you to complete the task. The 'client' might keep demanding more. I learned this the hard way when I first started.

Another point to consider is that if you don't value your work, why should a potential client?

A telltale sign is when a new potential client insists that your first piece of work should be free. They might argue that this is reasonable since they don't know you and aren't sure if you'll deliver.

If you feel compelled to accommodate them, offer a one-hour consultation, a first meeting, or some advisory or instructional information that will benefit them. Make it clear that if they want more after that, your time or service becomes billable.

Should you offer free?

If it can help you demonstrate your value to potential clients, then yes.

Many service professionals offer their first hour free. The goal is to understand the potential client's needs and for both parties to get to know each other. This also saves the service provider time and money by having the client come to them, and the client might be more inclined to proceed once they've made the effort to show up.

An initial meeting or call can go in several directions. It can uncover a need that wasn't apparent at first, which can be beneficial for both parties.

The meeting might excite the service provider, or conversely, they might decide it's not worth pursuing and the best course of action is to do nothing.

Ideally, an initial meeting could lead to a long-term relationship and a solid business deal.

Alternatively, you might refer the potential client to another service provider who you believe is a better match.

Free information

Free information can be delivered in various formats such as downloadable guides, interactive charts, posters, audio files, or videos. Typically, this information is centered around a specific topic or issue and is used to attract potential customers based on their interests. This could potentially lead to more significant opportunities.

From a new client's perspective, they are seeking a solution to their problem, and the provider that appears to have the answer is likely to be chosen. Providing quality information can lay the foundation for a strong relationship and lead to more significant opportunities.

As a provider, the free information you offer might be similar to what you would share in an initial meeting. Therefore, offering free information online can save time and, once created, the cost to distribute it can be minimal.

The design and delivery of your information are crucial. It should be clear, easy to understand, and include an offer. The language should be simple and avoid technical jargon if possible. The goal is to impress the reader with friendly, accessible, and straightforward information. Ideally, it should simplify a complex process or system.

The ultimate goal is to include an irresistible offer.

Service for free

Generally, working for free is not advisable, but there are exceptions, especially when it comes to bulk purchases. For example, offering a two-for-one deal where one item is free if a sale is made. Alternatively, you could offer a special discount of 50%, which could be adjusted based on your situation.

Gift Certificates

Offering redeemable gift certificates can be beneficial as they are typically pieces of paper with a value that can only be redeemed at your business. They can be used as a thank you for business or a reward for referrals. The goal is to encourage the recipient to spend the money. Gift certificates are effective in networking, retail, and on-site events.

Newsletters and magazines

Regularly providing clients with information through newsletters or magazines can be a great way to stay connected and show your relevance to maintain their interest. Customers often choose to do business with you because of shared values. They appreciate that you can do the work they need without them having to develop internal expertise, saving them time and usually costs as well.

Newsletters or magazines typically contain light yet impactful content that highlights points of interest within your field of expertise that are important to your clients. This shows your ongoing commitment and may remind your customers why they choose to do business with you.

Many businesses now distribute newsletters or magazines electronically, which can be less costly but may not be as widely read due to the volume of emails your clients receive. Printing and mailing hard copies can be more effective.

Having your own publication can also provide opportunities to maintain social connections with customers. Newsletters can celebrate social events and even include invitations to birthdays, trips, or other events. They can also provide entertainment such as puzzles and jokes. There is plenty of software available to help you create these.

Ongoing content strategies

To put it simply, publishing one article per week might be sufficient to fill a newsletter or generate a continuous stream of free content. Each article can be posted on your website to enhance your SEO. Creating weekly content allows you to engage with current events by commenting on recent news stories.

You can acknowledge the original source and reiterate key details, making sure not to copy the original content verbatim. The goal is to provide your personal interpretation or explain the relevance of the news to your audience.

There's always something new happening. Business sections or even Google can provide links to pertinent stories for you to analyze. References to these stories can be included in your newsletters and magazines.

Significant events are reported in newspapers daily, and it's entirely possible to connect your interests, skills, and accomplishments to ongoing issues like climate change. For instance, major networks like CNN have committed to focusing on climate change in the future, and other broadcasters seem to be following suit. Despite the cynicism, many people are interested in learning more about it.

Climate change has been an issue since the 1800s, and it's a story that has enduring relevance. It's a global issue that affects everyone. There's plenty of opportunity for everyone to contribute to the fight against climate change.

There are numerous other stories reported daily that might be more relevant in attracting potential customers. Starting a business can be triggered by any event. Many of us have interests, hobbies, or professions that others might share, which could be a good reason to start a business.

For example, my first legitimate business was born out of a home computer hobby I had when I was younger. In a short time, it turned out to be profitable. A quick anecdote: I once had a conversation with a dentist that led me to help other dentists transition from patient care to practice management. I didn't need to know anything about dentistry to provide this advice and get paid for it.

An experienced dentist can easily mentor other practitioners because they have decades of experience. It's a common trajectory, but many fail to see the potential to train others when they have industry experience. Even without expertise in a particular subject, you can still provide advice to those who do.

Starting a business doesn't require any specific experience. What you do need is a customer. Whether you're offering advice, digging holes, stacking shelves, or delivering goods, someone will compensate you. Anything is possible.

Start soon

When launching a business, many people spend money on unnecessary items. Do you really need business cards, a new phone, an office, a car, or a photocopier? Many of these expenses require a monthly commitment. You might be able to afford the initial payments, but the challenge is keeping up with them.

You need a consistent monthly income to cover these costs. Otherwise, your business could quickly become chaotic.

who are you working for?

Are you employed by yourself or a financial institution?

The perceived expense of starting a business often deters many. However, in the initial stages, most of these costs aren't necessary.

Office space can be rented by the hour.

Photocopies can be paid for as needed.

Transportation can be arranged through Uber.

Virtual assistants can be hired, and you only pay for the services you use.

Business cards can be designed affordably on websites like fiverr.com, and so forth.

I started my first business with nothing more than a borrowed bucket and sponge. As a teenager, I sought out customers within my immediate vicinity. The point is, you don't need to borrow money to start a business. You can borrow any resources you need to get going without spending a dime.

It's entirely possible to start from nothing and eventually consult with renowned brands and household names. I did it. I started from the ground up. The only thing I felt necessary to purchase was a suit.

If a business is viable, it will generate profit. Therefore, the real test of a business is its ability to make money. If you can't figure out what to charge for, you don't have a business yet.

Be patient, success doesn't happen overnight. You'll figure things out and eventually find yourself running a business.

There's a right time to invest money into a business, and the first investment should ideally be aimed at generating profits. We often invest in businesses hoping for a return on investment, but what if the business fails? How much should we invest or risk? The concept of a no money down business is to eliminate any initial risk by not investing any money upfront. This approach allows for greater flexibility.

Investing money often leads to a focus on recouping that investment. But what if your potential customers aren't interested in what you're selling?

Paid for learning

Restaurants are a common choice for family businesses. This is understandable, as everyone needs to eat and many families enjoy sharing their culinary skills. However, I've seen many families invest heavily in a restaurant only for it to go under.

Restaurants require significant capital for various reasons and usually involve a long-term rental commitment. You need to install a kitchen, stock perishable items, and furnish the dining area. These are all warning signs.

Regardless of customer volume, you're still obligated to cover staff wages, rent, and other ongoing costs. These expenses never cease and can quickly become overwhelming.

Running a successful restaurant is a commendable achievement given the challenges involved.

Business ventures that end up losing money are often categorized as paid for learning. If you have a steady income, you might be able to afford such ventures.

I've certainly had my share of paid for learning experiences. It's not ideal, but it happens to even the best entrepreneurs. It's also a difficult way to start a business. Not only do you need to recover your investment, but you also need to turn a profit. Why make things harder than they need to be?

My most successful ventures required no initial capital investment. However, there's a case for reinvesting profits to expand the business and stimulate growth. Banks are even willing to lend money to finance confirmed orders.

But to take on financial risk to grow a business initially is unnecessary. If your idea is good, customers will pay for it. It's as simple as that.

Other considerations include the type of business you're starting. Many people say they want to start an internet business. While this is a common sentiment, it's often misguided. The internet isn't a customer; it doesn't buy anything.

Your focus should be on how you can serve customers. The internet is a medium for conveying messages. Your customers will inform you of what those messages should be.

Once you've identified your target audience, find out which media they use regularly. If your audience can be reached via the internet, that's great. However, you don't want to be one of those entrepreneurs who've lost everything because they misunderstood how to use the internet for business.

By reading the next chapter, you could find yourself running a small business and generating income swiftly. All you need to do is implement a few of the ideas presented.

Chapter 2: Generating Business Concepts

Where do you begin when you have an idea? How does it function? And how can you apply it to the business you're planning to start? Let's be straightforward: business ideas emerge once you've identified what you want to do.

Starting a business requires substantial efforts such as developing a business plan, attracting investors, securing funding, and hiring employees. However, before you jump into these steps, the first and most important thing is to have a solid business idea. No matter how innovative or unique your product or service is, it must have a demand and people must be willing to pay for it. To come up with a great idea, you need to think deeply, use your imagination, and do extensive research. Here are some things to consider when trying to generate business ideas for your own venture.

How to Generate Ideas

Think about the products and services that could make your life better. Make a list of your unique skills and areas where you could improve. Look for potential solutions on that list that could enhance your life. Reflect on your personal experiences and spend time analyzing them. With enough thought and effort, you can certainly come up with numerous beneficial products or services.

Decide whether you want to offer a product or a service. The basis of a new business idea usually revolves around either a product or a service. Each choice requires careful thought and creativity. Before choosing one over the other, carefully weigh the pros and cons of each:

• If you plan to sell a product, it needs to be developed or improved before you invest in production. Creating and manufacturing new products can be expensive but potentially profitable if successful.

• On the other hand, offering a service eliminates the need for product creation and manufacturing. However, relying solely on providing a service may present difficulties in expanding your business, requiring the hiring of more staff. Regardless of the route you choose, investing time and resources in marketing and promotion is essential.

Identify a problem in a market segment where you have expertise. Have you recently bought a product that you think could be better in terms of quality? Were you unhappy with a certain service? Sometimes, dissatisfaction with current practices can inspire you to start a business or create something new. Keep an eye out for such problems as they occur, as they may signal a market need that you can meet. For example, if there are no bike repair services in your community, you've identified a need that you can meet by offering that service.

Adapt a proven business idea. Instead of focusing only on industry problems, you can also draw inspiration from companies that excel in a certain area. Look into whether you can improve on an existing idea and carve out your own niche in the market. Google is a perfect example of this approach, as it revolutionized internet search engines by developing a highly accurate algorithm for improved search results. Many successful companies and entrepreneurs have started by enhancing existing products or services. You can use this strategy too.

Consider future trends. Successful entrepreneurs are forward-thinking and anticipate emerging opportunities. By observing current trends and envisioning their logical progression, you can come up with unique ideas that could disrupt the market. For instance, as remote teaching becomes more popular, starting a company that focuses on tools to help remote teachers could be a game-changing idea. Analyzing current trends and advancing them can unlock untapped potential.

Conduct preliminary customer research. Although market research is typically done after ideation, conducting early studies can help you align your ideas with customer needs and wants. Find out what people are looking for by doing online research. Use search engine tools like Bing Ads or Google AdWords to identify popular keywords. Also, consider interacting directly with potential customers through face-to-face interviews or online questionnaires to gain insights into their preferences.

Use your expertise in a different field. Another way to generate new products or services is to leverage the skills you've gained from past experiences. Applying your expertise creatively in unrelated industries can often lead to breakthroughs. For example, Leo Fender, who started as a radio repairer, used his knowledge of electronics and engineering to revolutionize the music industry. By applying his expertise to guitar design and manufacturing, he created iconic instruments that forever changed how musicians play and express themselves. This example shows the power of using your existing skills and knowledge in a different field to generate innovative business ideas.

To further illustrate this concept, consider exploring industries unrelated to your expertise. Look for ways to transfer your unique skill set and perspective to new domains. For example, if you have a background in software development, you could apply your programming skills to create innovative solutions in the healthcare or financial sectors. By thinking outside the box and embracing interdisciplinary approaches, you can uncover unexplored opportunities and introduce disruptive ideas.

Furthermore, collaboration and networking can enhance the generation of business ideas. Engage with professionals from different industries, attend conferences and workshops, and participate in online communities relevant to your interests. By immersing yourself in diverse knowledge pools, you gain exposure to different perspectives and can identify potential synergies and partnerships that fuel creative thinking.

Remember, the process of generating business ideas is not confined to a single moment of inspiration. It's an ongoing journey of exploration, research, and refinement. Be open to feedback and continuously iterate on your ideas. Adopt the mindset of a lifelong learner, and let your experiences and interactions with the world shape and evolve your entrepreneurial vision.

By actively participating in the process of generating business ideas, you can discover unique opportunities, create valuable solutions, and make a lasting impact. The path to success begins with the spark of an idea and the determination to bring it to life. Embrace your passion, leverage your expertise, and embark on this exciting journey of entrepreneurship. Remember, the world is waiting for your innovative ideas. Let your entrepreneurial spirit fly, and together, we can shape a brighter future.

UNCOVERING IDEAS

Reflect on the goods and services that could improve your lifestyle. Make a list of your unique skills and areas where you need improvement. Evaluate if any of the listed items can enhance your life quality. Take time to ponder on your personal experiences. By dedicating time and effort, you'll certainly come up with a variety of beneficial products or services.

Decide if you want to offer a product or a service. The basis of a fresh business idea typically revolves around these two options: a product or a service. Both options demand careful thought and creativity. Before choosing one over the other, weigh their pros and cons:

- If you opt for a product-based business, think about the need to create or enhance the product if it already exists in the market.

- Offering a service eliminates the need for product creation and manufacturing.

- While creating new products can be expensive, successful ones can be very profitable.

- However, if you only offer a service, expanding your business can be difficult and may require hiring more staff. Regardless of the strategy you choose, investing time and resources in marketing and promotion is crucial.

Identify a problem in a market segment you are familiar with. Have you recently bought a product and found it to be of poor quality? Were you unhappy with a certain service? Sometimes, dissatisfaction with existing methods motivates people to start a business or create something new. Actively notice such problems to generate business ideas. Others might share your dissatisfaction, creating a market opportunity. For example, if there's no bike repair service in your community, identifying this gap presents an opportunity for you to offer that service.

Adapt an existing business idea. Instead of focusing on the current industry's shortcomings, you can observe companies that are good at what they do. Look for ways to improve their methods. By taking an existing idea and pushing it beyond what competitors do, you can create a unique market position. Google is a great example of this, improving an already successful concept. When Google started, there were several other search engines. However,

Google's precise algorithm greatly improved search results, leading to its outstanding success. Many successful companies or business owners have followed a similar path by enhancing existing products or services. You can do the same.

Consider future trends. Successful entrepreneurs are forward-thinkers who foresee future developments and use them to their advantage, instead of sticking to outdated methods or technologies. This could involve predicting a product line's logical progression or expanding services. By looking at current trends and advancing them, you can come up with a unique idea that could potentially revolutionize the market. For example, with the increasing popularity of distance learning, you could consider starting a company that specializes in tools for remote teachers. Develop an idea that's innovative and capable of transforming the industry.

Carry out preliminary consumer research. While market research is usually done after an idea has been formulated, you can still gather initial insights into consumer preferences. This will help you shape your concept based on the needs and wants of potential customers. Conduct online research to identify frequently searched keywords, as they can provide inspiration. Alternatively, services like Bing Ads or Google AdWords can provide more detailed data on popular search terms.

Use your skills in a different field. Another method for coming up with new services is to use your skills and expertise from a different field. Think about the knowledge and skills you have and see how they can be used in a different industry or context. This approach allows you to bring a fresh perspective and unique solutions to an existing market.

Brainstorm with others. Collaboration can be a powerful tool in generating business ideas. Have discussions with friends, colleagues, or mentors who have experience in entrepreneurship or different fields. Their insights and perspectives can ignite new ideas and help you refine your concepts.

Stay updated with new technologies and industries. It's crucial to keep track of new technologies, industries, or societal changes that could potentially disrupt current markets or provide new opportunities. Stay informed about advancements in areas such as artificial intelligence, blockchain, renewable energy, or biotechnology, and think about how you can use these advancements to create innovative products or services.

Focus on niche markets. Instead of aiming for broad markets, it might be more beneficial to concentrate on niche markets with specific needs and preferences. Identify customer segments that are underserved or overlooked and have unique needs. By serving these specialized markets, you can set yourself apart from your competitors and establish a loyal customer base.

Analyze successful business models. Investigate successful business models from various industries and pinpoint the key elements that contribute to their success. Look for patterns, innovative strategies, or gaps in their services that you can incorporate into your own business idea. This can offer valuable insights and inspiration for crafting your own unique concept.

Test your ideas. After you've come up with a list of potential business concepts, it's crucial to test them before investing substantial resources. Carry out market research, collect feedback from potential customers, and evaluate the feasibility and viability of each idea. This process of validation will assist you in identifying the most promising concepts and making informed decisions about which ones to pursue.

Creating a successful business concept requires a mix of creativity, market awareness, and research. By considering your own abilities and experiences, identifying market gaps or issues, modifying existing ideas, predicting future trends, collaborating with others, and staying updated about new technologies, you can come up with innovative and viable business ideas. Always remember to validate your concepts before proceeding, as this will enhance your chances of establishing a successful and sustainable business.

Chapter 3: initiating a business

Organizing Your Thought Collection

Even the smallest or most mundane ideas can hold great potential. Cultivate the habit of carrying an "idea notebook" to record your thoughts as they occur. Keep this notebook within reach at all times because inspiration can strike at any moment. By doing so, you can compile all your ideas in one handy location. Regularly revisit this notebook to pinpoint ideas that could be further expanded or refined.

You might want to transfer these ideas to a computer or phone, depending on your preference and accessibility, but a physical notebook is always a good alternative. This way, you have a backup in case your notebook gets lost or damaged. Digital storage also allows you to neatly organize and classify your ideas, which can enhance your creative thinking process. During brainstorming sessions, avoid being overly critical of your ideas. Give yourself the liberty to daydream and delve into various thoughts that come to mind. Use different techniques to stimulate your imagination and encourage idea generation.

To stimulate your creativity and motivation, regularly go for walks. Not only are these beneficial for your health, but they can also spark your imagination. Numerous studies have demonstrated the positive effects of walking on brain health, especially in terms of creativity. Carry your journal on these walks to jot down any insights or ideas that come to mind. Additionally, visiting local stores, especially large department stores, can provide inspiration. Casually stroll through the aisles and make a list of the products and services you see. Think about what improvements or modifications these items might need. Don't ignore hidden opportunities, as they can lead to potentially untapped but commercially viable ideas.

Broaden your perspective by interacting with people from various professions. If you're developing software, seek advice not only from fellow IT experts but also from professionals in other fields. Try new experiences and connect with unfamiliar people. Observe how they use products or services to improve their lives. This approach can inspire you to generate ideas from unique perspectives and innovative viewpoints.

Take short breaks to let your brain relax and generate ideas naturally. It's a known fact that many great ideas come to people when they are not actively looking for them. Step back from intense thinking and shift your attention to activities like reading, walking, watching a movie, or engaging in other enjoyable hobbies. Try not to think about your business, product, or service during this downtime. You never know when the solution to a nagging problem might suddenly appear.

Getting enough sleep is vital for maintaining a sharp and alert mind. Make getting a good night's sleep a priority to optimize your brain's performance. Keep a pen and notepad near your bed, as innovative ideas or solutions may come to you in your dreams.

ASSESSING YOUR IDEAS

Weigh the pros and cons of your plan. Even if you have an excellent idea, consider whether you have the resources to implement it successfully. For instance, starting a restaurant business might sound appealing, but you also need to consider whether you have the necessary experience or culinary training to make it successful.

Check if someone else has already thought of your idea. It's quite possible that if you've come up with an idea, someone else has already had a similar one. Research to see if your business idea has already been implemented. You wouldn't want to invest a lot of time and resources into developing an idea, only to find out later that someone else has already put it into action. Carry out an in-depth investigation to establish the uniqueness of your idea.

Begin with a web search engine, using relevant keywords to look for existing solutions or ideas. If you don't find an exact match, probe deeper to see if any businesses similar to yours already exist. Remember, this method can be more time-consuming and complicated, and you might need to consult a patent law expert to guide you through it effectively.

Research your competitors. If you discover that someone else has already thought of the same idea as you, don't be disheartened. Many new businesses face stiff competition when they start, but they overcome it by offering superior products or services. Thorough research of potential competitors is crucial.

Interact with your competitors' customers through formal or informal surveys. Ask them about their satisfaction and dissatisfaction with the competitor's services or products. This will help you modify your business operations to cater to their needs. Look into your competitors' online presence, including their blogs and review websites, to find out their weaknesses or criticisms.

Before seeking customer feedback, discuss your idea with trusted friends, family, and colleagues. Explain to them the benefits your idea can bring to the market. Ask for their honest opinions and whether they would consider buying your product or service. Their initial evaluation can provide valuable insights, be it positive feedback, constructive criticism, or potential issues. Take all feedback into consideration, regardless of its nature.

Interact with potential customers to measure their interest in your idea. After discussing your concept with close friends and believing in it, extend your reach to see if there is a customer base for your business. Try different methods to see if people would be willing to use your products or services.

Conduct in-person interviews with individuals who could be potential customers. For instance, if you're creating a new fishing lure, speak to employees in the fishing section of various sports stores. Share your potential business idea and ask about their interest in that particular market segment. Keep these conversations short to respect their time.

Consider sending questionnaires via email using tools like Google Forms. Distribute these surveys among your personal contacts and ask for their feedback. Also, encourage them to share the surveys within their networks.

Identify and assess potential risks and challenges related to your plan. Every business plan has risks, be it financial or emotional. Anticipate these hurdles and think about how you can tackle them to increase the chances of successfully managing potential threats and sustaining your business. Here are some tips to overcome common obstacles:

Collaborate only with reliable individuals to prevent negative effects on your business.

Always evaluate your financial resources before proceeding. Insufficient funding is a major reason for startup failure.

Be willing to adapt to market changes to remain competitive.

View failure as a learning experience, and be ready to adjust and improve your strategy.

Ensure that your plan is practical and executable. Think about various factors and consider them carefully before committing to your idea. Here are some things to think about:

Reflect on the survey and interview results you've gathered. Is there a market for your idea?

Be honest with yourself and avoid unrealistic expectations if there's limited interest from potential customers.

Assess the competition level and devise a detailed strategy to outperform competitors.

Analyze the costs related to your plan, including both startup and ongoing expenses. Evaluate the economic feasibility of your idea and check your available financial resources.

Estimate the expected expenses and potential income related to your plan.

Arrange your ideas in order of best to worst. After addressing the previous points, assess each idea's performance. Prioritize them with the most promising one at the top. This ensures that your efforts are concentrated on developing your best idea. Ideas at the bottom should either be discarded or significantly improved before considering implementation. To ensure the success of your shoe business, it's essential to accurately identify your target market. Assuming that every person on the street is a potential customer is unrealistic. Instead, concentrate on a smaller target market, like middle-class teenagers. Start by figuring out the percentage of children from middle-class families in your country, as this will give you an idea of the potential customer base.

Next, think about the specific shoe needs of your target audience. Investigate what types of shoes are popular among middle-class teenagers. Do they prefer sporty shoes, trendy sneakers, or formal footwear? Knowing their preferences will aid in customizing your products to meet their demands effectively.

Assess the current market situation to see if it is expanding or remaining the same. Look at existing research on the shoe industry and carry out your own unique study. This research could include interviews, customer surveys, or other methods to gather useful information. Also, evaluate the competition level in the market. Find out the market share already owned by other shoe companies and the number of competitors you will be up against.

To gain a competitive advantage, plan your strategies for distinguishing yourself from other market participants. Examine the pros and cons of potential competitors and identify how your business can stand out. This analysis will help you understand what makes your products or services unique and beneficial to your target customers. It is vital to clearly show how your customers will benefit from choosing your business over others.

Detail your product or service. Highlight the unique features and benefits that make your offerings attractive to customers. Start by defining the problem your product or service solves and then explain your solution. Give an overview of how your product or service fits into the larger market context. Investigate what other companies are already offering solutions to this problem and underscore the elements that make your offering different from theirs.

In this section, detail each managerial and operational role within your business. Describe the organizational structure, remembering that it can be changed later. Assign roles and responsibilities to individuals or groups in charge of different business aspects. If you haven't hired staff yet, recognize the gaps and outline the tasks for those roles. Each team member should have a brief profile that highlights their relevant experience or qualifications for the role.

Create a detailed sales and marketing plan. Start by conducting an in-depth market study and defining your target buyer personas or ideal customers. Decide how you plan to penetrate the market and plan your strategies for business growth. Prioritize the most effective distribution channels and describe how you will interact with your customers.

Address questions about your sales strategy, growth plans, sales team structure, average sale price, and the number of sales calls needed to finalize deals. Expand on your pricing strategy and provide a thorough financial plan, including estimated costs, funding needs, and projected revenue. If you're seeking investors, present your financial plan clearly, including start-up costs, cost forecasts, and a funding request.

By following these steps and using the advice given, you can create a thorough business plan that covers all the vital aspects of your shoe business and sets you up for success in the market.

To figure out the initial costs of your business, you need to estimate the expenses for the resources required to set up your business and the actual cost of acquiring these resources. Think about whether you need to rent an office space or need a computer. It's essential to give honest and reasonable estimates for these factors and their related costs to prevent running out of funds.

To get funding for your business, list your expenses and provide accurate financial estimates to back them up. Making sure your financial model is correct is vital to increase your chances of getting funding from investors and credit sources.

You might want to consider adding an appendix to your business plan. Although it's not compulsory, it's a good place to include any relevant attachments like rental agreements, licenses or authorizations, legal documents, cover letters, professional profiles of team members, and resumes of co-founders.

Picking a name for your company is a big decision. The name will be used in official documents and in the business plan you present to investors. It's recommended to develop your strategy first before deciding on the name. Here are some strategies for naming your company:

Create a list of potential names: Use traditional brainstorming to come up with different name options. For local businesses, adding the city name to the service offered can improve local search results. But if you're starting a creative or unique business, go for a unique and memorable name that fits your brand.

Do a trademark search: Before you decide on a name, do a trademark search to make sure it hasn't been registered or requested by another business. Misusing a trademark can lead to legal problems, so it's important to do your homework.

Check availability in your state: Make sure the name you want isn't already being used by another company in your state. Business name registrations are usually specific to each state, but trademark issues can occur if the name is already trademarked.

Check domain name availability: Think about how the chosen name will look as a website domain. Make sure it's short, memorable, and easy to type. Check with domain name registrars to see if the domain name you want is available. Register the domain quickly to secure it.

If you've chosen a unique name, you might want to register it as a trademark for extra protection. Trademarks give owners exclusive rights to specific words, images, and logos related to their products and services.

Including the name of your business is optional and usually happens naturally during the registration process. But if you do business under a name different from your registered name (this applies to sole proprietorships, partnerships, corporations, or existing LLCs), you might need to submit a "Doing Business As" (DBA) name application. You can complete the application process at your state government or county clerk's office, depending on where you are.

If you're not sure about business structures like LLCs, corporations, or partnerships, don't stress. These are different types of legal entities that determine how your company is managed from the top down. We'll talk about how to choose the right structure later on.

SELECTING THE APPROPRIATE BUSINESS FRAMEWORK

When launching a business, it's crucial to decide on a legal structure that aligns with your needs and influences your liabilities and tax obligations. The four most prevalent business structures are corporations, limited liability companies (LLCs), sole proprietorships, and partnerships. This guide will assist you in determining the most suitable ownership framework:

SOLE PROPRIETORSHIP (SINGLE-OWNER BUSINESS) A sole proprietorship is a business solely owned and managed by one person. The business and the owner are not legally separate. Here are some advantages and disadvantages:

Advantages: Establishing a sole proprietorship is straightforward and cost-effective, with the owner having complete control over all business decisions. Tax filing is simpler as the owner's personal and business taxes are merged.

Disadvantages: The owner is personally responsible for all the business's risks and liabilities. Raising funds or attracting investors or loans can be difficult due to the lack of a separate legal business structure.

Consider a sole proprietorship if you plan to be the only employee in the near future and are comfortable bearing the entire financial responsibility for the business.

PARTNERSHIP A partnership is a business model with two or more owners who contribute to all aspects of the business and share its profits and losses. Here are some advantages and disadvantages:

Advantages: Establishing a partnership is relatively simple and less expensive. It allows for resource pooling and access to diverse skills and knowledge.

Disadvantages: Similar to a sole proprietorship, partners are personally liable for the business's risks and liabilities. Disputes between partners can occur, making it crucial to have a formal agreement in place.

Consider a partnership if you plan to start the business with someone else and are comfortable sharing the liability and working collaboratively.

LIMITED LIABILITY COMPANY (LLC) An LLC is a business model that provides its owners with limited liability protection while maintaining flexibility and simplicity. Here are some advantages and disadvantages:

Advantages: LLC owners have limited personal liability for the business's debts and liabilities. It is easier to manage than a corporation with fewer formalities and regulations.

Disadvantages: Compared to sole proprietorships and partnerships, LLCs can have higher startup costs. Some venture capital funds may be reluctant to invest in LLCs due to tax implications and complexity.

Consider an LLC if you want limited liability protection and prefer a business model that is less complex than a corporation.

CORPORATION A corporation is a separate legal entity from its owners, offering the most protection but also the most complexity. Here are some advantages and disadvantages:

Advantages: The personal assets of the owners are protected from the company's debts and liabilities. Corporations can easily attract venture capital and offer the best asset protection.

Disadvantages: Corporations have more intricate tax and legal regulations, leading to higher administrative costs. C corporations are subject to double taxation, and there are more formalities and regulations to follow.

Consider a corporation if you have secured enough venture capital or have a larger, more established business with several employees.

SETTING UP YOUR BUSINESS After deciding on the most suitable business structure, it's necessary to legally establish your business and adhere to all legal requirements. Here's how to go about it:

1.   Choose your business location: Pick the state where your business will be based.

2.   Register your business name: By forming an LLC or sole proprietorship, the business name is automatically registered. Alternatively, you could use a "Doing Business As" (DBA) name.

3.   Acquire an Employer Identification Number (EIN): If you're not a sole proprietor or a single-member LLC, you'll need to get an EIN from the IRS.

4. Meet additional legal requirements: Depending on your business type and location, you might need to acquire business licenses, permits, or certifications.

5. Understand or look for investments from venture capitalists or angel investors. Here are some steps to consider when seeking funding for your business:

6. Identify your funding needs: Determine the amount of capital you need to launch and maintain your business. Develop a detailed budget that includes your expenses, such as equipment, inventory, marketing, and operational costs.

7. Utilize personal resources: Think about using your personal savings or assets to finance your business. This could involve using your personal savings account, leveraging home equity, or selling non-essential personal assets.

8. Reach out to friends and family: Consider asking close friends and family members to invest in your business. Show them your business plan and financial forecasts to illustrate the potential return on investment.

9. Small business loans: Look into and apply for small business loans from banks, credit unions, or other financial institutions. Prepare a detailed business plan, financial statements, and collateral (if necessary) to back your loan application.

10. Government grants and programs: Look into government grants, subsidies, or programs that support small businesses. These vary by location and industry, so research options specific to your business.

11. Venture capital and angel investors: If your business has high growth and scalability potential, consider seeking investment

from venture capitalists or angel investors. These investors provide capital in return for equity or a share in your company. Prepare an engaging business pitch and seek opportunities to connect with potential investors through networking events or pitching competitions.

12.   Crowdfunding: Consider crowdfunding platforms where individuals can donate funds to support your business. Develop an engaging campaign that showcases your business idea, value proposition, and rewards for contributors.

13.   Strategic partnerships: Look for strategic partnerships with established companies or organizations in your industry. They might be interested in providing funding or resources in exchange for a mutually beneficial relationship.

14.   Bootstrapping: Think about bootstrapping your business, which involves funding it with your own revenue and profits. This strategy requires a lean and cost-effective operation to generate enough cash flow to sustain and grow your business over time.

15.   Remember, each funding option has its own benefits and considerations. Carefully review the terms, potential impact on ownership and control, and repayment requirements before committing to any funding source. Also, consult with financial advisors or professionals to ensure you make informed decisions.

By combining the right legal structure with the appropriate funding strategy, you can create a solid foundation for your business's success.

Chapter 4: The Best Business Model criteria

Many business owners struggle to achieve success, with numerous ventures hovering on the brink of collapse. However, a handful of businesses not only manage to stay afloat but also flourish for extended periods, consistently raking in significant profits. What makes these businesses different? The secret lies in their foundation - their business models.

This chapter is dedicated to revealing the art of designing profitable business models, which are the bedrock of lasting success. We will pinpoint the main features that separate successful businesses from short-lived ones. Whether you're an entrepreneur, a business owner, or someone considering entrepreneurship, understanding the principles behind these exceptional models can offer you a roadmap to success in your venture.

By delving into the key takeaways, you'll gain insights that challenge traditional views on entrepreneurship. From the crucial role of Lifetime Client Value (LCV) in generating sustainable revenue to the importance of securing external capital, each takeaway is a valuable piece of the puzzle in building a profitable business.

As we examine the various traits of a successful business model, you'll discover the intricacies of predictable cash flow, the strength of niche specialization, the appeal of high entry barriers, and the potential for scalability. Using real-world examples and practical insights, this chapter arms you with the tools to evaluate and select the right business model for you, guiding you towards a path of prosperity.

Whether you're an experienced entrepreneur looking to fine-tune your business strategy or a budding visionary taking your initial steps in the entrepreneurial world, the lessons in this chapter are universally relevant. Here are some ideas to help you establish a foundation for sustainable growth, lasting value, and ultimately, a journey towards success that defies the odds.

1. The Significance of Choosing the Right Business Model:

A business model serves as the roadmap to success for any venture. It outlines how a business generates, delivers, and captures value. The choice of model is crucial as it sets the direction for your business. A well-crafted model integrates your resources, customer segments, and revenue streams, promoting stability and growth.

2. Emphasizing Lifetime Client Value (LCV):

Lifetime Client Value represents the total value a customer brings to your business throughout the entirety of your relationship.

Companies that focus on LCV aim to establish enduring relationships, often through subscription-based or long-term contracts. This approach leads to steady cash flow and improved customer retention, reducing the need for continuous customer acquisition.

3. Ensuring Predictable Cash Flow and Revenue Streams:

Predictability is a desirable quality in business. Models that provide recurring services, subscriptions, or long-term contracts guarantee a stable cash flow. This financial stability acts as a buffer against market volatility, facilitating better financial planning and resource distribution.

4. Attracting Investor and Fund Interest:

When a business model attracts interest from investors and funds, it indicates its potential for growth and profitability. A robust model draws external capital, expediting expansion and boosting credibility. Investors value the promise of steady cash flows and the prospect of predictable returns.

5. Creating a High Barrier to Entry:

A high barrier to entry prevents competitors from easily mimicking your business. Models that offer unique value propositions, proprietary technology, or specialized expertise establish protective barriers around the business, enabling you to set higher prices and sustain profitability.

6. Concentrating on Niche Markets and Specialization:

Niche businesses serve a specific market segment, establishing strong ties with their audience. Specialization allows for customized products or services that deeply resonate with customers, fostering brand loyalty and reducing competition.

7. Adhering to Regulation and Standardization:

Business models operating within regulated sectors enjoy a level playing field. Regulations establish guidelines that all competitors must adhere to, curbing market volatility and ensuring stability. This factor can foster a conducive environment for sustained profitability.

8. Ensuring Scalability and Exit Strategy:

Scalability refers to a model's capacity to expand without a corresponding increase in costs. A scalable model appeals to investors and prepares the business for mergers, acquisitions, or public offerings. The possibility of an exit strategy enhances the model's attractiveness.

9. Adopting Diversification and a Portfolio Approach:

Operating multiple profitable business models to diversify risk associated with market fluctuations is a prudent strategy. Merging models with different customer bases, revenue streams, and industries can result in a more robust business portfolio.

10. Prioritizing Long-Term Vision and Sustainable Growth:

Profitable business models are designed for longevity. Their emphasis on stable revenue streams and enduring customer relationships aligns with sustainable growth. Such models can withstand economic downturns and set businesses up for long-term success.

11. Conducting Research and Due Diligence:

In-depth research is crucial before settling on a business model. It's essential to understand the market, competition, customer needs, and regulatory environment. Due diligence helps minimize risks and ensures you're entering a market with growth potential. Regular research, which is a tax-deductible expense, can help keep the business competitive.

12. Embracing Adaptation and Innovation:

The business landscape is constantly changing, requiring adaptability and innovation. Even with a profitable model, ongoing adaptation to shifting customer preferences, technological advancements, and market trends is essential to stay relevant and successful.

Remember, these key points are interlinked. Constructing a profitable business model involves understanding and integrating various elements to form a comprehensive strategy that promotes long-term success.

Here are 40 businesses that utilize certain business models to varying degrees. It's important to note that not all businesses will perfectly match every characteristic, and the success of each business model can depend on a variety of factors. Some of these businesses may require initial capital to get started, often for things like deposits and initial rent payments. You may also need to put in some work yourself and enlist the help of friends and family to get things off the ground. However, due to their inherent qualities, these businesses are likely to be sustainable and minimize risk.

1. Day Nurseries: Operating a day nursery can provide a good average lifetime value as customers usually stay for several years. This business model also benefits from upfront payments, providing a steady cash flow. It's also a regulated industry, leading to standardized competition. Additionally, this sector often attracts investors, making it potentially profitable.

2. Private Preschools/Kindergartens: Similar to day nurseries, private preschools also offer a stable income due to long-term students and upfront payments.

3. Food Services Business: Providing food services to large groups like offices, factories, and schools ensures regular and repeat customers, leading to predictable cash flow. This stability makes it an attractive model. Additionally, this sector often attracts investors, indicating its potential profitability.

4. Event Catering Companies: These businesses operate on contracts and offer consistent business from clients who need catering for their events.

5. Contract Catering: Similar to food services, contract catering involves providing food for schools, factories, or office blocks on a contract basis. This offers even more predictable revenue since the customer base is well-defined and contracts are typically long-term.

6. Commercial Property Rentals: Investing in commercial properties and renting them out can provide stable rental income, especially if the property serves as your business location. This model benefits from tax efficiencies and can be relatively resistant to economic downturns.

7. Shared Office Space: Renting out office spaces to multiple businesses offers a steady income stream from long-term contracts.

8. Commercial Storage Facilities: Providing storage solutions to businesses can lead to recurring revenue and long-term contracts.

9. Commercial Hygiene and Waste Services: These businesses offer steady demand and revenue. They tend to be recession-proof and can attract investment interest due to their predictable nature.

10. Commercial Cleaning Services: Like hygiene and waste services, cleaning services offer recurring contracts for maintaining cleanliness in commercial spaces.

11. Medical Practices (Dentists, Doctors): These professional services have high lifetime client values due to long-term patient relationships and repeat visits.

12. Legal Firms: Another example of professional services with high client values due to ongoing legal needs and long-term relationships.

13. Accounting Firms: Similar to legal firms, accounting services offer ongoing value with regular financial management and tax assistance.

14. Financial Planning Services: Providing financial advice and planning services can lead to long-term client relationships and high lifetime values.

15. Commercial Landlord: Owning and renting out commercial properties offers consistent rental income from long-term leases.

16. Physical Therapy Clinics: Like medical practices, physical therapy clinics offer ongoing services and long-term patient relationships.

17. HR Consulting Firms: Providing human resources consulting services to businesses involves long-term relationships and contract-based work.

18. Veterinary Clinics: Veterinary services offer long-term client relationships and repeat visits for pet care.

19. Educational Tutoring Services: Providing tutoring services can lead to long-term relationships with students and parents.

20. Fitness Studios: Memberships and class packages can provide predictable income from regular attendees.

21. Subscription Box Businesses: Offering niche products through subscriptions creates recurring revenue from loyal customers.

22. Commercial Landscaping Services: Providing landscaping and outdoor maintenance to businesses involves recurring contracts for ongoing services.

23. Commercial Waste Management: Like hygiene services, waste management companies offer predictable income from contracted services.

24. Printing and Signage Services: Printing and signage companies can build long-term relationships with businesses for their branding needs.

25. Childcare Franchise: Running a franchise of a childcare center provides a proven business model with high potential for profit.

26. Home Care Services for Seniors: Providing in-home care services to seniors involves long-term client relationships and regular services.

27. Language Schools: Offering language learning programs can lead to ongoing relationships with students.

28. Fitness Equipment Rental Services: Renting out fitness equipment to businesses or individuals can create recurring income streams.

29. Employee Training Programs: Offering corporate training programs involves long-term relationships with businesses seeking professional development.

30. IT Support Services: Providing IT support to businesses leads to recurring contracts for ongoing tech assistance.

31. Commercial Pest Control Services: Pest control companies can secure ongoing contracts for maintaining a pest-free environment.

32. Architectural Firms: Designing and planning services involve long-term projects and relationships with clients.

33. Commercial Real Estate Brokerage: Brokering commercial real estate deals can result in significant commissions and long-term clients.

34. Business Coaching/Consulting Services: Offering coaching or consulting to businesses can lead to high-value long-term relationships.

35. Child Enrichment Centers (Art, Music): Enrichment centers for children offer long-term programs with regular attendance.

36. Corporate Wellness Programs: Offering wellness programs to companies involves long-term contracts and recurring services.

37. Corporate Event Planning: Event planning for businesses provides contracts for organizing various corporate events.

38. Executive Search Firms: Providing executive recruitment services leads to high-value contracts and long-term relationships.

39. Medical Billing Services: Handling medical billing for healthcare providers involves ongoing services and long-term contracts.

40. Educational Publishing: Creating educational materials can lead to consistent sales to schools and educational institutions.

Chapter 5: Financing Your Business

Raising capital for starting a business or expanding an existing one is essential. Depending on your business type, there are several methods you can use to gather the needed capital. Some people use their own savings, while others prefer to take loans (debt financing) or sell shares in their company (equity financing). Other innovative ways include using credit cards, crowdfunding, or purchase order financing.

Applying for a Business Loan

1.	Find suitable lenders: Business loans are a commonly used method of financing. Reach out to banks you have a relationship with and ask about their business loan application process.

2.	Small Business Administration (SBA): The SBA, while not a lender itself, offers loan guarantees for small businesses. This means if you fail to repay the loan, the SBA will cover the repayment. Remember that the definition of a "small" business varies by industry.

3.	Online lenders: Online lenders often have more relaxed loan conditions and might not ask for collateral. However, it's crucial to check their credibility by reaching out to the Better Business Bureau and local consumer advocacy groups.

4.	Prepare necessary paperwork: Lenders need to evaluate your business's financial health before granting a loan. Get ready with the following documents that most lenders usually ask for:

o   Resumes of owners and management

o   Business and personal tax returns for the past three years

o   Personal and corporate bank statements

o   Credit reports

o   Company licenses

o   Articles of organization or incorporation

o   Commercial leases

5.   Keep financial reporting current: Most lenders also require financial information from your business. Make sure the following are prepared and regularly updated:

o   Personal financial statements certified by major business owners (generally those owning more than 20% of the business)

o   Company balance sheet (overview of assets, liabilities, and owner equity)

o   Income statement (shows company profitability over a certain period)

o   Cash flow analysis

o   Check and correct any errors in your credit report before applying for a loan

6.   Provide collateral: Offering assets as collateral can make loan approval easier, especially if you don't have a credit history. Various assets like property, vehicles, equipment, or other valuables can be used as collateral. Talk to banks to understand their specific requirements and appraisal procedures.

7.   Submit loan application: After you've submitted your application, the lender will review it and make a decision. This

process usually takes two to four weeks. If you've applied to several lenders, compare loan details such as interest rates, fees, prepayment penalties, and repayment schedules.

Looking for Investors

1. Identify suitable investors: Raising capital for your business can be achieved by selling shares of your company. It's crucial to identify potential investors that align with your business needs. There are various types and sizes of investors to consider.

o   Colleagues: Think about collaborating with colleagues who have the necessary skills you require, such as expertise in marketing or product development.

o   The general public: Publicly traded companies offer the opportunity for the general public to buy shares. To explore this avenue, it's advisable to consult with a securities attorney as it involves dealing with the Securities and Exchange Commission.

o   High-net-worth individuals: Angel investors are affluent individuals who invest in start-ups. In exchange, they often expect a seat on the board of directors or involvement in daily operations.

o   Venture capital firms: These firms assess and invest in businesses, often playing an active role in decision-making and company expansion.

2. Grasp the advantages and disadvantages of equity financing: By selling a portion of your business, you acquire more shareholders who are eligible for future profits. They may also have voting rights in company decisions and unrestricted access to your business information.

o   If you relinquish more than 50% of your company, you might lose control, but the upside is that you won't need to repay the funds if your business fails.

How to Fund Your Business

Section 1: Ways to Fund Your Business

Capital is crucial for initiating and growing your business. Depending on your unique business requirements, there are several methods to generate the required capital. While using your own money is a typical financing approach, other well-known alternatives include debt financing (borrowing money) and equity financing (selling shares of your business). Additionally, innovative tactics such as using credit cards, crowdfunding, or purchase order financing can also be explored.

Section 2: Securing a Business Loan

Securing a loan is arguably the most prevalent method of financing a business. Here are some steps to guide you:

Identify potential lenders for businesses:

a. Commercial banks: If you already have a business account with a bank, you can approach them and inquire about obtaining a business loan.

b. Small Business Administration (SBA): Despite not being legally allowed to lend money directly, the SBA offers loans for small businesses, meaning they will cover the cost in the event of a default. However, eligibility for SBA loans can differ based on your industry type.

c. Online lenders: Online lenders often have more flexible loan criteria and may not require collateral. However, it's crucial to investigate the lender's credibility through resources like the Better Business Bureau and local consumer protection agencies.

Prepare the necessary paperwork:

Lenders need specific documents to evaluate your company's financial health before approving a loan. Ensure you have the following documents:

Resumes of owners and management

Business plans

Personal and business tax returns for the previous three years

Personal and business bank statements

Credit reports

Business licenses

Articles of organization or incorporation

Commercial leases

Keep your financial records updated:

Most lenders will also request financial information from you. Make sure to create and regularly update the following records:

Personal financial statements certified by major business owners

Company balance sheet, outlining assets, liabilities, and owner equity

Income statement, illustrating the company's profitability over a certain period

Cash flow analysis

Review your credit report and rectify any mistakes before applying for a loan. Errors can include incorrect balances, credit limits, or accounts inaccurately reported as being in collections or default. Rectify errors by reaching out to the appropriate credit bureau either online or by mail.

Securing a Loan with Collateral:

One way to obtain a loan more easily, particularly if you don't have a credit history, is by using assets as collateral. These assets could be your home, car, equipment, or other valuable items. You should talk to various banks to understand their specific requirements, which may include property appraisals.

Applying for a Loan:

Once you've completed your loan application, the lender will review it and make a decision. This process usually takes between two to four weeks. If you've applied with multiple lenders, make sure to compare the terms of each loan, including interest rates, fees, early payment penalties, and the length of the repayment period. Before finalizing your decision, consider the overall cost and terms of each loan. Make sure all the necessary details are accurate and don't hesitate to reach out to your loan officer if you have any questions. Don't forget to submit all the required supporting documents along with your application.

Section 3: Attracting Investors:

Another method to raise funds for your business is to attract investors. Here are some steps you can follow:

Choosing Your Investors:

First, you need to decide on the kind and size of investors you want to attract. Your options could include:

Colleagues: You could consider partnering with a colleague who has skills that your business needs, such as marketing, product development, or sales.

Public: If your business is publicly traded, the general public can buy shares of your company on the stock market.

Angel Investors: These are individuals who typically provide capital in the early stages of a business in exchange for equity or convertible debt.

Venture Capitalists: VC firms invest in businesses with high growth potential in exchange for equity. They usually invest larger sums than angel investors.

Preparing Your Pitch:

Create a concise and persuasive pitch that showcases the unique selling points, growth potential, and financial projections of your business. Clearly explain what makes your business stand out from the competition and how investors can benefit from investing in your company.

Networking and Attending Investor Events:

Attend networking events, industry conferences, and startup competitions to meet potential investors. Build relationships and seek introductions to investors through mutual connections or professional networks.

Creating an Investor Presentation:

Create a comprehensive investor presentation that outlines your business model, market analysis, competitive landscape, financial projections, and funding requirements. Use visual aids like charts and graphs to effectively communicate your message.

Pitching to Investors:

Arrange meetings with potential investors to present your business and investment opportunity. Be ready to answer questions about your business strategy, market potential, revenue projections, and expected return on investment. Highlight the key benefits and risks associated with investing in your business.

Negotiating Terms and Closing the Deal:

If an investor shows interest, negotiate the terms of the investment, including the equity percentage, valuation, and any additional conditions or agreements. Seek legal advice to ensure the terms are fair and align with your business goals. Once both parties agree on the terms, finalize the investment through legal documentation and the transfer of funds.

Section 4: Exploring Different Ways to Finance Your Business

In addition to traditional bank loans and securing funds from investors, there are other ways you can finance your business:

Crowdfunding:

Crowdfunding websites provide a platform for you to gather money from a large group of people who each contribute a small amount. You can showcase your business idea or project on these websites and offer rewards or incentives to encourage people to support you. Some well-known crowdfunding websites include Kickstarter, Indigo, and GoFundMe.

Applying for Business Grants:

You can look for and apply to grants provided by government bodies, non-profit organizations, or private companies. These grants are usually given based on certain criteria such as the industry you're in, your location, or the social impact of your business. Be aware that the application process for grants can be rigorous and competitive.

Financing from Suppliers or Vendors:

Some suppliers or vendors may be open to providing financing options to assist you in purchasing their products or services. This type of arrangement allows you to delay payment or establish a payment plan.

Bootstrapping:

Bootstrapping involves funding your business using your own personal savings, credit cards, or the revenue from initial sales. While this approach requires careful financial management, bootstrapping allows you to retain complete control of your business without taking on debt or giving up equity.

Remember, the method of financing you select should align with your business objectives, financial requirements, and risk tolerance. You may want to consider getting professional advice from financial advisors, lawyers, or business consultants to help guide you through the process.

Chapter 5: The importance of no money down

Starting a business without any initial capital is a completely different ball game compared to starting one with money. Having too much capital can actually pose a problem. If you start with a lot of money, there's a higher chance of wasting it, especially if you're funding a personal, ego-driven idea. With money in hand, you might feel invincible and believe that all you need to do is execute your plans to succeed. However, the fundamental aspect is managing the business to generate more money, adhering to the principle that money begets money.

People who find themselves in this position are usually very committed to their mission. They adopt an all-or-nothing attitude, believing that if they're going to do it, they should do it right. This mindset was prevalent during the dot com boom, where every idea was considered a surefire success. Everyone seemed to be making fortunes, but in reality, most were spending their family wealth in the perceived dot-com boom.

When the dot-com bubble burst in 2001, it resulted in nearly $8 trillion in losses. As a service business, we lost some clients, but most of our clients were banks and well-known retail and travel companies like Disney that had an online presence as part of an existing business. Fortunately, we maintained a diverse client base and didn't lose many.

One business that I won't name was a website based on a popular TV show at the time. The family running the website was related to the TV show's producer, and they were fully invested in the project. They had the advantage of using the show's design, branding, video clips, voices, and images. The website was promoted on the TV show, and it was very popular, with thousands of new users signing up every day.

My agency's role was to drive more traffic to the site. We ensured it was easily discoverable by search engines and optimized for speed. The site was managed by a highly competent and dedicated team. It was a great case study, but there was one major issue - it wasn't making enough money. The family had invested a lot into it, even re-mortgaging their house.

They were always investing in the next big thing, like a top-of-the-range CRM with an integrated shopping cart. The site did generate good revenue, but I'm not sure if it was enough to provide a return on investment. The owners always assured me that everything was going well and they were good at paying their bills.

I enjoyed working with them, and they seemed to like me too. They often invited me to their launch events and even hired me to speak at their events to confirm the traffic figures. However, after many years, the TV show ended and the site was shut down.

It seems they were unable to turn their venture into a profitable enterprise and chose to withdraw discreetly. I believe they simply decided to minimize their losses. They were, after all, people of integrity.

I attribute their failure to their insistence on only purchasing the best and newest items, likely coupled with a plethora of monthly subscriptions. Their business management style differed significantly from mine. It's crucial to establish a business on a solid customer base, where we either turn a profit each month or scale back our operations. Even though it was a tough decision, it was the only viable option.

Their business model was based on a television show, and they correctly predicted that it would drive traffic that could be converted into sales. They did receive a lot of traffic and made some sales. I have a hunch that the sheer volume of traffic they received each month may have given them hope that they would generate the necessary sales in the subsequent month. In the meantime, they continued to incur expenses and increase their monthly costs. It appears they reached a point where they realized their efforts were not yielding returns and decided to cease operations, having exhausted their time.

Clues on what to sell

As a provider specializing in traffic, we informed our clients about the source of their website traffic and what their visitors were looking for. The search terms used by visitors gave us hints about what products they might be interested in buying. However, we didn't handle our clients' finances or business strategies. Our role was to provide advice, make suggestions, and offer assistance. Throughout our years-long partnership, we didn't notice any issues with revenue. In fact, it seemed like our client was running one of the most successful websites on the internet, based on the data we had access to and their own reports.

The sales process is relatively straightforward. You can figure out what the market is interested in based on their behavior. In this case, it was home cooking. Everything related to home cooking was selling well, from cookware and cutlery to books and other products. All of these items could have been tested. A few phone calls could have been made to check prices and inventory, and then offers could have been made to see what garnered the most interest. They also had the chance to offer high-end, branded products. They could have used the show's logo and the stars of the show to promote these products. I'll never understand why they didn't take full advantage of these opportunities.

Over the years, I've met many people in the industry who were part of a family that started a website. Many of them ran into financial troubles, but they used their newfound knowledge to find jobs working for others. They were likely hoping to make a comeback in the digital world someday.

I know many people who went to the city with a business plan but didn't get the funding they were hoping for. A few lucky ones did get funding, and they seemed to follow a similar path to mine. My business was a supplier to gold miners, but we didn't do the mining ourselves. There were many service companies emerging, all eager to help customers improve sales, usability, and user behavior tracking. It seemed like everything could be managed and organized.

The city provided us with customers. There was plenty of money available for the gold miners. Various trends came and went, from community and health to fitness, pets, fintech, and more. Everything was becoming virtual, and it felt like a revolution had taken place.

Our website was our storefront, and we were the top result in search engines for many years. Our sales figures were impressive as well. Customers are everything to us.

Many new businesses had great ideas, but few knew how to effectively attract customers. Most believed in the "build it, and they will come" approach.

My goal was to attract customers who would make purchases. My test was simple: does a customer want to buy what we're selling? If not, what do they want to buy? They're buying something, so let's keep trying different offers until they buy from us.

Our main customer came to us by chance through a referral, and they weren't even in the city. The sales director learned about what we could do from a conversation with his ex-wife, who worked for another one of my businesses. He spent our first meeting telling me what he wanted, and we agreed that we could deliver. As a result, he placed an order, and we had to quickly figure out how to fulfill it. And we did.

It was clear to me what had to be done and the way to do it. But it wasn't until I made my first order that I truly began to work towards accomplishing the necessary tasks. This wasn't about pretending until success was achieved. Rather, it was about securing a customer before making a larger investment. Simply put, you don't have a business until you have a customer. Ideas are plentiful, but customers are scarce! Only when we understood the customer's needs could we start to consider how to meet them.

While others were focused on selling website design, we were intent on delivering what the customer wanted. We discussed potential outcomes and results, and invited customers to tell us what they wanted. We knew what had been successful in the past, and now we're enjoying the process of working with clients and delivering the service.

We documented the case study and even created a few hypothetical use-cases to show what could be achieved. We cautiously offered the service to other marketing directors, and some were eager to take us up on it.

The work was highly technical, but we hinted at it without going into too much detail. Our marketing and communication efforts emphasized the expected outcomes and results.

Supply is easy, but demand is the real challenge. We could direct many people to relevant websites to provide information and cater to their interests. The tricky part is converting them into customers. We aim to provide a brand experience that aligns with their purchasing desires, not before. Otherwise, we risk creating a brand experience for a brand with no customers, which is pointless, even though many business owners invest upfront thinking it's crucial. The key is to understand if customers are interested, how they will make their interest known, and how we can facilitate the process.

The first step when you have an idea is to evaluate it as quickly and cost-effectively as possible.

We need to be agile and precise, both online and offline, in all aspects.

You've probably heard the term "new and exclusive." This is because the offer is new, and it's exclusive because only one is available. If something is being promoted, it's possible to create another and another. Each item can be designed exclusively until it's not.

At each testing stage, you can modify the offer. You can adjust the price point, alter the design, change the exclusivity, take into account feedback and reviews, and so on.

3 things you can test fast

Testing the market doesn't have to be expensive.

For a cash-strapped start-up, there are three things you can quickly test. You can provide personal services, share information, or sell a finished product.

Personal services involve you performing a service for your customer. The initial costs are usually zero. You just need to show up. If you make a sale, you could potentially hire someone, effectively financing the sale. If possible, financing sales is generally a good strategy. You can always take a loan for this, as you'll get the money back.

When it comes to information, this typically involves providing guidance or instructions in the form of a book, digital document, or coaching service. You likely already have most of the resources you need. The main task is to compile everything and present it in an appealing way. This can yield significant returns, allowing you to quickly turn a small investment into a larger profit.

If you're selling a finished product, you'd typically use materials you already have or can easily acquire or manufacture. Initially, you might do this as a side job to meet the needs of your primary customers. This could continue until you run out of materials or the side income surpasses your main job's income.

Any of these three options could be a suitable path for most people, and this is often how a business naturally starts to grow.

You'll likely need some money to finance growth and pay for services over time. But initially, with no money, growth might be slow. However, this isn't necessarily a bad thing.

Having a backlog of customers is great. It gives you a chance to explain to potential customers that your prices need to increase based on what you've learned from your initial customers. They can choose to go elsewhere, or you can offer two prices: a higher price for quick turnaround (which may require upfront payment) and a lower price for those willing to wait. Alternatively, you can stick to your original promise and build a reputation for reliability and integrity. The choice depends on what makes the most sense given the circumstances.

Your initial customers might be the lucky ones, as you may be willing to serve them at any price just to prove you can support some customers.

One way or another, you'll get to where you need to be.

Financing actual customer sales is less risky and burdensome than funding an unproven business. When you're financing sales, you're past the start-up phase and on your way to growth.

Needing money to finance sales might seem challenging and even embarrassing, but it's also a sign of success. If customers want to buy from you faster than you can deliver, that's a good problem to have. Often, the solution is to raise prices to cover costs and compensate for the risk and additional financing costs associated with financing sales through delivery.

Yes, I've made errors, absolutely! Even when my goals were clear, I sometimes ended up hiring the wrong people or paying for services and equipment that weren't effectively used. However, I refrained from taking out loans and entered into very few financial agreements.

88 | P a g e

I was once hit hard by a photocopying contract that my co-director signed while I was on vacation. I was furious, although it initially seemed like a wise decision. But eventually, as anticipated, it backfired.

I was obliged to pay monthly rentals and storage until the end of the photocopier contract. The cost wasn't exorbitant, so it was merely a minor annoyance, but ultimately a wasteful expense.

In the end, I became the owner of this troublesome machine and sold it to a church for ten dollars. Otherwise, I would have had to pay five hundred dollars to have it scrapped.

I've invested and lost small amounts of money. I've spent over a year on projects, investing my time and effort, only to gain nothing. The lesson here, which I knew but somehow overlooked, is that the only way to validate a business is to see if customers will buy what you're selling. I occasionally fell into the trap of believing that if I built it, they would come.

This flawed philosophy has been at the root of many failures, and yet, I felt compelled to follow it.

The major mistake I made was becoming overly cost-conscious, trying to do more and more work myself.

It's good to be mindful of costs, but it's also important to factor in the cost of time.

Think of time as part of the expense (time equals money). Nevertheless, there were some positives. One of them was the lesson I learned. I also managed to gain qualifications in the process, discovering skills that I could get certified in, like being an agile project manager.

These newly acquired and certified skills opened doors to entirely new markets. After a year of hard work, this led to some unexpected financial rewards.

Lean business principles

Lean business principles and agile development, typically used in software companies, advocate for the creation of a minimum viable product (MVP). This principle can be applied to any business, not just software ones.

In today's world, a website can be quickly set up as an MVP. The cost of creating a website is minimal, with the domain name often being the most expensive part. However, even domain names can be obtained for free with careful searching. By using server-less technologies and doing it yourself (for example, hosting on Amazon s3), monthly website costs can be reduced to a minimum. If the business venture does not succeed, server-less cost models eliminate ongoing monthly costs due to lack of traffic.

A website serves as an effective platform to showcase an MVP. It allows for the exchange of ideas and the opportunity to attract visitors. Different strategies can be tested to convert these visitors into customers. The beauty of this technology is that it can often be implemented with little to no cost. The success or failure of the MVP depends on the strength of the offer, not the cost of the supporting technology.

Banks often provide financing for customer-based growth. However, start-ups can gain an advantage from having little to no cash to invest, as this reduces the risk of losing money. By carefully allocating each cost and investing only in what is needed, you can get exactly what you want.

The 5 steps to success with no money down:

1. A product or service

2. A market strategy. Understanding who your customers are and why they would buy your product or service.

3. A passion or interest in the subject that can keep you motivated over time.

4. The energy to implement your plans. This requires taking care of your physical and mental health, as well as maintaining a balanced diet.

5. The ability to take action. This is often the most challenging part as many people fail to follow through.

Here are three essential lifestyle principles to remember:

1. Be mindful of how you manage your time.

2. Cultivate a sense of responsibility.

3. Always act in accordance with your beliefs.

Time management is crucial. To be productive, you need to work smarter, not harder. This may mean cutting down on leisure activities like watching TV or going out to socialize, if permitted by your local regulations. As social beings, we enjoy spending time with friends and family. However, to achieve your business goals, you have to invest time in planning, strategizing, and refining your business model. You need to ensure your business thrives and your family is well taken care of.

Try to visualize how your business will evolve over time. Instead of dreaming about filling your bank account, focus on the process and the details of each step. When you do this, you'll find that the money will naturally follow. Consider your target customers, their buying patterns, and how you can incentivize them to buy more or recommend your products or services. It's an interesting exercise that involves thought, not necessarily cost. If costs arise from your thoughts, evaluate if they are necessary and if they can be delayed.

The second principle is embracing responsibility. Your success is solely your responsibility. It's futile to blame external factors like relationships, economic conditions, government policies, or competitors. These are common challenges that every business owner faces. You're not alone in this journey. The goal is not to choose between running a business and maintaining your relationships. The goal is to find a balance that allows you to do both. This might involve some compromises, but taking responsibility will guide you through these challenges.

Starting a business can be a daunting task, especially if it's your first time. But remember, you're not alone. Millions of people have started businesses before you, and you can learn from their experiences. Balancing your work and family life can be tough, but it's crucial to involve your family in your decisions and make time for them. After all, your ultimate goal is to provide a better life for them.

The third principle is belief. If you don't believe in what you're doing, or if you don't think it works, or if you don't like your customers, then it's best to stop. If you continue without belief, you're likely to fail. On the other hand, if you believe in your mission, you'll have hope and expectations, and you'll find the strength to persevere. If a business strategy or process conflicts with your beliefs, discard it and find an alternative that aligns with your values. Internal conflict can drain your energy and undermine your belief in your mission. If the means don't justify the end, find a better way. Stop, rethink, retool, and restart.

Note that money is not a prerequisite for success, nor is it mentioned in any of these principles. I've found that money usually comes from customers. If you take care of your customers, they will take care of you.

When you hit a financial roadblock, remember that you have several alternatives to consider. For example, you could license a successful product or service in your local area to a distant region. Licensing can provide a steady stream of income without the need for sales financing, and it can be marketed as an asset class.

Many businesses don't make money for a long time, often because they only have one source of income. However, there's no rule that says you can't establish additional income streams to attract more customers. For example, you could monetize certain marketing channels, write and sell a book on Amazon, run a YouTube channel, or operate a membership site. These and other marketing channels could potentially generate substantial income.

It's crucial to diversify and create multiple income streams as soon as possible. If you rely solely on one income stream, you're vulnerable if that source encounters problems. It's also important to balance sales and marketing with production and delivery; if you're always delivering, you won't have time to sell. As a guideline, I suggest spending no more than 30 minutes to a few hours each day on marketing activities.

If you're considering starting a YouTube channel, be prepared to create a weekly video and not see any income from traffic for possibly up to two years. If you're producing a product on your own, it could take a year or more to start making money. With a partner, it could take weeks or months. If you're providing a service, it could take just one successful meeting to secure a trial contract.

I always encourage my clients to pay monthly retainers whenever possible. This allows me to plan ahead and increases the likelihood of success. Ongoing monthly contracts are valuable and many clients are happy to sign them because they offer price stability and predictability.

When starting a business, I would advise against hiring anyone right away. Treat the new venture as a side hustle and invite friends to join you on the chance that it might succeed. Always ask customers to pay at least 50% upfront and to provide written orders.

Offering a money-back guarantee can be a good idea, but I've only ever done it with online sales where it's required. If a customer is unwilling to pay any money upfront, you might end up with a client who never pays. Asking for money upfront is often necessary to ensure the customer is committed and to build trust.

Another important consideration for start-ups is to avoid offering services for free. It can make you appear desperate and unlikely to deliver quality work. If you only get business because you offer services for free, you're not respecting the market's value.

Requiring a written order from a customer is important for several reasons. It can serve as proof to suppliers, banks, and partners that you have a customer. It can also help define expectations and ensure both parties understand exactly what is to be delivered.

Finally, remember that small steps can lead to big leaps. It's time to give yourself a raise and a promotion!

Chapter 6: Gaining new clients to expand your customer base

As a seasoned entrepreneur, I've faced my fair share of obstacles and understand the critical role that new customers play, especially during lean times. In this chapter, I'll share my personal journey and insights on launching and expanding a business, even in the most difficult of circumstances. Writing a book was never part of my initial plans, but I'm excited to share my expertise with budding entrepreneurs like you.

The process of attracting and persuading potential customers to choose your product or service over competitors, known as customer acquisition, is a fundamental aspect of any business. It necessitates a well-planned strategy to draw in leads, cultivate them, and ultimately convert them into loyal customers. The cost associated with these activities, referred to as the client acquisition cost (CAC), is an important factor to consider.

For businesses of all sizes and stages, attracting new customers is paramount. It not only generates the revenue needed to maintain operations and facilitate growth, but it also serves as a testament to your success, attracting potential partners, investors, and influencers. Consistently attracting and converting new customers not only pleases investors but also enhances your business's overall reputation.

Customer acquisition allows you to create a systematic plan to draw in customers and ensure your business's longevity. Relying on organic customer growth is an option, but it doesn't guarantee steady profits over time. This is where customer acquisition specialists step in, employing specific strategies to encourage potential customers to act.

It's crucial to understand that customer acquisition extends beyond traditional marketing. While marketing raises awareness, customer acquisition seeks to inspire action. For example, marketing analytics can measure the success of a Facebook ad campaign targeted at your desired audience. However, acquisition refers to the actions potential customers take after interacting with your ads, visiting your website, or engaging with your emails. The moment a customer decides to make a purchase signifies successful acquisition, contributing to your business's revenue.

You might be curious about the distinction between lead generation and customer acquisition. To understand this, let's delve into the concept of the customer acquisition funnel, a model commonly used in the business world to map out the customer journey.

As customers move through the funnel, they become increasingly aware of your brand, consider your products or services for potential purchase, and ultimately decide to do business with you. Lead generation, lead acquisition, and lead conversion occur at various stages of the funnel. However, it's crucial to view the entire process of attracting and acquiring customers as the comprehensive customer acquisition funnel.

Acquisition marketing is a strategy that focuses on creating ad campaigns that target consumers already familiar with your brand and considering a purchase. It sets itself apart from other advertising forms by focusing on converting prospects who are already aware of your business.

In the modern digital era, digital acquisition marketing is increasingly important. It uses online channels like display ads, social media, and organic search to attract and target new customers. A successful digital acquisition strategy requires close collaboration between your marketing and customer service teams.

Your marketing team crafts and disseminates persuasive promotional materials to pique the interest of prospective clients. Simultaneously, your customer service staff, who interact directly with your existing customers, can also significantly contribute to attracting and retaining new clientele. The collaboration between these teams ensures that your customer acquisition marketing efforts go beyond traditional marketing boundaries.

Alongside organic search and digital strategies, companies employ various customer acquisition methods like email marketing, organic social media, and paid advertising. Each method has its unique advantages and is effective under different circumstances. Knowing your target audience, resources at your disposal, and overall business strategy will guide you in selecting the most effective acquisition strategy for your business.

Organic search, or SEO (Search Engine Optimization), involves enhancing your content to achieve a higher ranking on search engine results pages (SERPs). By focusing on relevant keywords and producing engaging content, you can draw in potential customers who are actively looking for products or services similar to yours. Tools such as Open Site Explorer, SEMRush, and Ahrefs can assist you in identifying the perfect keywords for your business and improving your organic search visibility.

Pay-Per-Click (PPC) advertising is another beneficial paid search marketing method. With PPC, you design targeted ads that appear alongside organic search results. By bidding on keywords related to your business, you enhance your visibility and the likelihood of being found by potential customers. Platforms like Google Advertising and Microsoft Advertising offer tools to fine-tune your PPC campaigns and improve their performance.

Acquisition marketing also takes advantage of the digital world, using channels like social media and display ads to attract and engage new customers. By harnessing the power of social media platforms and generating compelling content, you can increase brand awareness and capture your target audience's attention. Cooperation between your marketing and customer service teams ensures a smooth experience for potential customers, whether they're browsing your website, interacting with your live chat, or reaching out through social media.

As you delve into various customer acquisition methods, it's crucial to strike the right balance between paid and organic strategies, inbound and outbound tactics, and available resources. Your acquisition strategy should resonate with your target market's preferences and behaviors and be flexible enough to adapt to changing market conditions and trends.

In this section, I've imparted valuable insights into customer acquisition, drawing from my successful entrepreneurial experiences. By grasping the principles of customer acquisition, reducing costs, and maximizing your existing clientele's value, you can devise a flexible and effective acquisition strategy that propels your business forward.

Remember, acquiring new customers isn't just about increasing revenue; it's also about fostering lasting relationships and laying a robust foundation for future growth. By investing in customer acquisition and consistently delivering value, you can position your business for long-term prosperity.

Now, equipped with this knowledge, it's time to take action and commence your customer acquisition journey. The opportunities are limitless, and I'm eager to witness the growth and success you'll attain. Let's dive in and acquire those new customers who will drive your business's expansion and pave the way for a brighter future.

Organic Social Media Platforms

As an established entrepreneur and expert in customer acquisition, I've had the opportunity to explore various strategies within the dynamic field of social media marketing. In this section, I'll delve into the subject of organic social media platforms, sharing my personal experiences and insights on how to effectively use these platforms for customer acquisition.

Social media marketing can be divided into two types: organic and paid. Both types have their benefits, but organic social media offers unique avenues for increasing brand visibility, developing a business persona, and sharing existing content from other sources like blogs or videos. It's like adding fuel to a fire that's already been lit through other acquisition strategies.

One of the main benefits of organic social media is its potential for viral content. By encouraging your customers and followers to share your brand's news, you can harness the power of word-of-mouth marketing. It's amazing how a single share can dramatically increase your reach and attract new customers.

However, depending on your budget and target audience, using paid social media platforms might be a better fit for your business. Investing in social media ads and visibility ensures you reach your target audience without needing to build a large fan base. While building a fan base is still crucial, paid social media can give your customer acquisition efforts an extra push.

To efficiently manage and schedule your social media content, I suggest using a free calendar template and management tool. This will help you stay organized and maintain a consistent presence on social media platforms.

Sponsored posts on social media do more than just deliver content. They allow you to collect useful user data like names and email addresses from your audience. This information is more than just content delivery; it helps you differentiate between a potential customer and a follower. Platforms like Facebook Lead Ads can be crucial in obtaining valuable leads for your business.

Email marketing, although considered outdated by some, is still an incredibly effective strategy for customer acquisition. It offers a direct line to your customers' inboxes, enabling you to communicate and convert them effectively. Through email, you can provide high-quality content, product details, discounts, and event updates. It also serves as a platform for meaningful interactions with your target audience, whether it's sending a birthday message or a thought-provoking marketing email.

Unlike other marketing channels like search or social media, email marketing provides a direct communication line with your customers. It's one of the most powerful customer acquisition methods, second only to direct sales. To leverage email marketing effectively, you need to build an email list and use it as a potent marketing tool.

Referrals, often overlooked as a source of customer acquisition, can be a game-changer. Your existing customers are the key to attracting new ones. While you can't force your current clients to refer others, you can foster an environment that encourages and rewards them for doing so. Setting up a referral program is a proven way to gain more customers through recommendations. By offering rewards and incentives, you can encourage your customers to promote your brand. Ensure the value you offer in return aligns with the importance you place on a customer referral.

Events, such as conferences, webinars, and trade shows, provide excellent opportunities to meet potential clients and grow your business. In today's digital world, virtual events have become more common, making it easier to acquire customers who register with their email addresses. Hosting virtual summits or webinars, or renting a booth at a larger event, can be a strategic step in your customer acquisition process.

Even though digital marketing is now the main focus, traditional marketing methods such as TV, radio, and print media are still relevant. These channels can be extremely effective for both small and large businesses, as long as you strategically target your advertisements. For instance, TV commercials allow you to reach a broad audience and use the power of visual storytelling. This can be especially powerful for brands that want to display their products or create emotional connections through engaging narratives. Radio provides a chance to connect with listeners through audio ads, which can be useful for targeting specific demographics or geographic regions.

Print media, including newspapers, magazines, and direct mail, can also play a crucial role in your marketing strategy. They provide a physical and trustworthy platform to communicate your brand's message and reach audiences who prefer reading offline. Print ads can be strategically positioned in publications that cater to your target market, ensuring your message gets to the right people.

When considering traditional marketing methods, it's important to thoroughly examine your target market, their media consumption habits, and the effectiveness of each channel. Moreover, combining traditional and digital marketing strategies can create a comprehensive and unified approach, maximizing your reach and impact.

Keep in mind, the effectiveness of traditional marketing channels may vary based on your industry, target audience, and budget. It's vital to monitor and measure the results of your campaigns to determine their ROI and make data-driven decisions about your marketing mix.

In conclusion, while digital marketing is crucial in today's connected world, traditional marketing methods like TV, radio, and print media still have a role. By understanding your target audience, customizing your message, and selecting the right channels, you can use the power of traditional marketing to supplement your digital efforts and achieve your marketing goals.

Now, let's talk about organic social media—the lifeblood of contemporary marketing. As a business owner, I've seen firsthand the tremendous impact it can have on businesses. In terms of social media marketing, there are two distinct types: free and paid. Today, I want to delve into the world of organic social media and examine how it can drive your business's growth.

Organic social media is all about increasing brand awareness, infusing personality into your business, and sharing valuable content that already exists elsewhere in the digital world—like your blog or videos. Consider it as adding fuel to a fire that you've already started using other acquisition strategies. It enables you to tap into the viral effect, encouraging your clients and followers to spread the word about your brand organically.

However, we shouldn't overlook the power of paid social media. Depending on your financial means and target market, using paid platforms may be a more strategic choice for your business. Investing in social media visibility and ads ensures that your message reaches your audience without the need to painstakingly build a following of devoted fans (although, let's be honest, that's important too).

To optimize your social media activities, it's essential to be organized and plan ahead. There are plenty of free tools and calendar templates available to help you manage your social media content more efficiently. Make use of sponsored posts to not only deliver your content to the right audience but also collect important user information such as names and email addresses. Facebook Lead Ads, for instance, are a powerful tool for promoting your content on social media, while also growing your contact list—a crucial step in distinguishing between potential leads and mere followers.

Email marketing, although considered old-fashioned by some, remains a highly effective customer acquisition strategy. It enables you to maintain a connection with your audience, providing them with quality content, product details, discounts, and updates on events. Email bypasses the limitations of search and social media algorithms, and content saturation, providing a direct line to your customers' inboxes. It's the second most effective method of acquiring customers, following direct sales.

So, what do marketers do with all the customer data they gather from various acquisition strategies? They compile an email list and utilize it as a powerful marketing tool. Email marketing offers unmatched opportunities for interacting with your target audience. Whether it's sending personalized birthday messages or informative marketing emails, it's a platform that allows you to customize your communication to cater to each customer's specific needs.

Referrals are a potent tool in your customer acquisition toolkit. Often, the most effective strategies are hidden within your existing customer base. One of the best ways to attract new customers is by leveraging customer referrals. While you can't force your current clients to recommend you, you can create a conducive environment that encourages and rewards their endorsement.

Setting up a referral program is an effective way to gain more customers through word-of-mouth. By offering incentives such as credits, tangible gifts, or cash rewards, you inspire your customers to share your brand. If you place a high value on a customer referral, be sure to reciprocate with something of equal value. B2C businesses often succeed with structured, reward-based referral programs, while B2B companies may benefit more from directly asking for customer referrals. Regardless of the approach you take, always prioritize delivering value before asking for anything. Give your customers a reason to endorse you, and when they are satisfied with your products or services, they will naturally become advocates for your brand.

Events serve as an excellent platform for meeting potential clients and securing new business. Conferences, webinars, and trade shows provide great opportunities to engage with your target audience. Despite the prevalence of digital communication in today's world, face-to-face interactions still hold immense value. Events allow you to display your products or services, engage in meaningful discussions, and build personal relationships with prospective customers.

To maximize the benefits of events, begin by identifying the conferences, trade shows, or industry events that cater to your target audience. Research the attendees, topics, and participation opportunities. Decide whether it's more beneficial to attend as an exhibitor, speaker, or sponsor, based on your objectives and budget.

When participating in events, ensure your booth designs are eye-catching, your presentations are engaging, and your materials are informative. Create a welcoming environment that piques the interest of attendees and encourages them to learn more about your brand. Provide interactive experiences, demonstrations, or samples to leave a memorable impression.

Building connections is vital at events. Engage with industry experts, potential clients, and influential figures. Participate in discussions, listen attentively, and exchange contact details. After the event, follow up with personalized emails or phone calls to further nurture these relationships.

Remember, events are not only confined to physical gatherings. Webinars and virtual conferences have grown in popularity, providing a convenient and cost-efficient way to reach a broader audience. Utilize technology to host webinars or participate in virtual events, broadening your reach and connecting with potential clients globally.

In conclusion, organic social media, email marketing, customer referrals, and events are all effective customer acquisition strategies. By strategically using these methods, you can increase your brand's visibility, build genuine relationships, and ultimately enhance business growth. Seize the opportunities offered by digital platforms, while also acknowledging the importance of in-person interactions. Tailor your approach based on your target market, industry, and available resources, and consistently assess and improve your strategies to maximize your customer acquisition efforts.

A sustainable approach to client acquisition is one that ensures long-term success. It involves investing resources such as money, time, and personnel in a manner that can be maintained in the long run. Let's delve deeper into this concept with some examples.

For example, suppose you choose to use a blog as a strategy to attract more customers. To guarantee its long-term effectiveness, you need to have the necessary resources and tools to regularly publish valuable content that generates organic traffic for weeks, months, or even years. Inbound marketing is a perfect example of a sustainable approach as it continuously attracts visitors and maintains a consistent influx of new customers. On the other hand, commercials may be effective in attracting customers in the short term but lack long-term sustainability.

Adaptability is key in the ever-evolving marketing landscape. With constant changes in consumer behavior and market dynamics, having a flexible client acquisition strategy is essential. In the past, salespeople were the main source of product information, but today, consumers are more skeptical of brand claims. Relying solely on salespeople for customer acquisition can be risky. By keeping your strategy adaptable, you can continually adjust it to align with changing market conditions and evolving consumer preferences.

Understanding your target market is crucial for successful customer acquisition. Not every customer is your ideal customer, so if your efforts are not directed at the right audience, they can end up being a waste of resources. Before investing in any client acquisition methods, it's important to define your target market. Creating buyer personas can help you eliminate inefficient or unnecessary acquisition efforts and better understand the specific needs and preferences that certain channels can meet. Taking a step back to establish a targeted customer acquisition strategy allows you to make informed decisions that align with your business, resources, and audience, resulting in measurable outcomes.

Diversifying your client acquisition approach can bring substantial benefits. Similar to how cross-pollination results in stronger plant species, diversifying your acquisition strategy and using a variety of approaches increases your chances of reaching new audiences and generating new leads. It also balances risk and reward, making it easier to shift investments to a different, higher-performing strategy if one channel underperforms.

Evaluating the lifetime value of each customer is vital for sustained success. While drawing in new customers is essential, maintaining their loyalty is even more significant. Recognizing the customer categories that demonstrate high loyalty can enhance your overall plan and the effectiveness of your customer acquisition initiatives. Customer lifetime value (CLV) pertains to the expected net profit that a person or business will generate throughout their tenure as a paying customer. Although computing CLV can be complex, it offers valuable insights into customer habits, directs marketing endeavors, and impacts business choices. Customers with a high CLV may initially cost more to acquire, but they surpass other customers in terms of revenue generation, referrals, and feedback. This allows for a more efficient use of their acquisition budget, leading to a greater return on investment and improved business outcomes.

By tracking CLV along with customer acquisition cost (CAC), businesses can ascertain the time required to recoup their investment in new customer acquisition, facilitating more informed decisions and resource distribution.

In summary, implementing a sustainable customer acquisition strategy requires investing in approaches that can be sustained over a long period. Having the necessary resources, adapting to evolving market trends, understanding your target audience, diversifying your strategy, and tracking customer lifetime value all play a part in crafting a successful customer acquisition strategy that delivers enduring results.

Chapter 7: Think big, Start small, Scale fast

Freedom at last

Start by jotting down your business ideas and thoughts, no matter how outlandish they may seem. It could be a simple list of things you're passionate about. There's no need for it to be organized or coherent at this stage; the important thing is to get your ideas out there. You can always refine them later. Once you embark on your entrepreneurial journey, you'll be your own boss. It's crucial to choose a line of work that you enjoy, as your enthusiasm will drive you forward.

Throughout your life, you've been taught what to learn and how to think. But now, it's time to break free and focus on what you truly want. That's why writing down your thoughts is so important. Your future is about you and your desires.

The dark side

You'll encounter naysayers who'll tell you that you can't succeed, that you're out of your depth, or that you don't deserve your independence. If you're offering business or technical advice, you might wonder who you are to advise a client or CEO. You may even face resistance from your family, particularly if they've always been employed by someone else or have a long history of working for the government.

You might also witness the inefficiencies of bureaucracy, such as wasteful spending on failing public utilities and poor return on investment. You might feel targeted by debt collectors, who often operate on the assumption of guilt until proven innocence.

There will be challenging times filled with doubt, frustration, and unhappiness. But these periods are usually short-lived, especially if you enjoy what you're doing. Consider starting a business in an area you're passionate about. This enthusiasm will be invaluable during tough times.

If you've been in a particular profession for a long time, like dentistry or law, and enjoy running a practice, consider transitioning to consulting. You could help other professionals in your field manage their practices or attract new clients.

Above all, remain optimistic. When one door closes, two more often open. It's not the obstacles that matter, but how you overcome them. When something unexpected happens, ask yourself: how can I make this work?

In the beginning, it's natural to take setbacks personally. But dwelling on them only holds you back. Instead, accept that things can go wrong and move on. If there's blame to be assigned, accept it and take responsibility. The sooner you address issues, the quicker you can return to the things you enjoy. Realize that you can often buy your way out of problems.

When things go wrong, don't waste time assigning blame. Accept it, move on, and find a solution. As long as money is coming in, you can pay your bills and keep moving forward. Remember, everyone encounters difficulties, especially entrepreneurs.

Most people in business are good people. Keep this in mind during tough times. Stay strong, don't give in too early, and be prepared for unexpected challenges.

How To Think Big, Start Small And Scale Fast

Everyone has the capacity to dream big, but in most cases, we don't immediately launch into large-scale operations. We usually begin on a small scale, aiming for incremental achievements. The quickest way to scale up is by convincing customers to pay in advance. With the prevalence of online transactions, people are accustomed to paying upfront for products and services. The most significant growth in recent years has occurred in the online sector.

Starting small typically means we aim to impress a select few with our skills or talents. Once we've impressed one person, it's easier to believe there are others out there who would also appreciate our offerings. Thus, we initially target a small audience.

Even if we have a grand idea, like creating an internet sensation with massive potential, it's still wise to start small. By dealing with customers on a one-on-one basis, we can gather feedback and adjust our offerings accordingly.

It's crucial to invest time in developing a high-quality, reliable product or service that will satisfy customers and keep them coming back. This way, we can gradually expand our business to meet growing customer demands.

Without a solid product or service, you may quickly find yourself in a difficult situation. Initially, you'll probably only cater to a few small clients. To expand, you'll need to significantly modify your offerings. Your first clients are likely to be risk-takers, eager to try something new. These early adopters, who enjoy being at the forefront of innovation, may make up about 20% of the market.

Over time, your clientele will become more mainstream, making up about 60% of the market. These customers are less interested in personal connections and more focused on getting the job done.

Then there are the laggards, who make up the remaining 20% of the market. These customers demand proven products with solid guarantees and are willing to pay the lowest price. They may not be your favorite customers!

You'll find that some customers, from all three groups, will stick with you for many years. Each group invested in you for different reasons. The first group may notice many changes in you and might even reminisce about the old days.

You'll need to identify and manage each customer group based on their perceptions of you. If you stray too far from these perceptions, they might start looking for alternatives.

It's crucial to retain past customers, or else you might just be paving the way for your competitors to step in.

Given these considerations, mass marketing can be quite tricky. Take Intuit, one of the largest online software suppliers. Despite its large scale, Intuit focuses a lot on small-scale interactions. They have a program where they work closely with customers to understand their usage and gather feedback to continually improve their software.

You might think there are exceptions to these principles. Consider Kentucky Fried Chicken (KFC), a global fast-food chain. Despite the numerous KFC outlets and other fast-food chains selling similar products, it's challenging to protect most businesses from being copied. Even KFC's 'special' recipe hasn't stopped others from selling similar chicken products.

I personally prefer smaller markets with a few frequent spenders, rather than large markets with many occasional spenders.

However, if you look back in history, even these massive chains started as single outlets.

Who are you for?

There exist several niche groups that possess remarkable purchasing power. It's a smart strategy to pinpoint these specific groups, as it can help you maintain their loyalty in the long run. Ideally, you want your customers to perceive you as their go-to choice.

Catering to a specific group demands a suitable level of personalization, which can help you stay as the top pick in your market. You can create tailored resources to generate exclusive intellectual property (IP) specifically for them. Essentially, this approach allows you to create a protective barrier around each customer group, making it challenging for your competitors to infiltrate.

Once you determine your target audience, you'll gain insights into their specific needs. This focus will enable you to showcase specialized knowledge that potential customers can identify and appreciate. Customers always favor 'insiders' as they believe it to be more efficient for them. If you can prove your understanding and proficiency, your target audience will rely on you to guide them towards success.

Your expert knowledge, skills, and experience can help keep customers loyal, as they won't want to miss out on what you offer. You can leverage this inherent allure to make it hard for customers to replicate your business unless they have a license.

Licensing is one of the quickest ways to expand. It's a win-win situation for everyone involved. It offers two major benefits: it's a cost-effective marketing strategy, and it's typically confidential. These two advantages are particularly beneficial for any start-up. It optimizes revenue and profits without revealing your trade secrets.

These principles can be adapted and implemented in almost any business. They are commonly used in most start-up ventures or market opportunities, with a few exceptions.

Avoiding Risk

Venturing into high-value markets, which are worth millions, often involves significant risk and incredibly slim profit margins. With such large sums of money at stake and such small profit margins, the pressure can be immense. The smallest mistake could result in you having to cover the loss. This high-stress environment leads many to abandon certain business ventures, primarily due to the substantial amount of money at risk.

While large sums of money may be attractive to those who seek prestige, smaller customer projects can often yield more profit with less risk. By spreading smaller amounts of money across a larger number of customers, the impact of a potential disaster is significantly reduced. While it's always best to avoid losses, a small loss would only result in a temporary, minor decrease in profits, as opposed to a catastrophic loss.

In essence, you can lead a less stressful and less risky life by diversifying your client base and focusing on low-risk projects. Otherwise, you might find yourself years into a business where a single, high-stakes gamble could wipe out all of your previous profits.

It's also important to diversify your business activities. Start by focusing on one area that interests you, then expand into one or two additional markets. For example, if you're interested in monetizing a podcast, you could:

• Choose a subject you're passionate about and target three related audience groups.

• Offer three types of products: a basic package, a monthly subscription package, and a premium package, each at different price points.

• Keep the content of each package largely the same, with only minor changes to suit each target market.

Take some time to think about how you could monetize a podcast using this model, then challenge yourself to implement your plan. This approach doesn't cost anything and can help you create a more appealing offer in several ways. It can also significantly increase your chances of success and reduce your risk.

By diversifying your client base, marketing strategies, and delivery methods, you'll quickly find out where your potential clients are and create multiple streams of income, reducing your risk. Monetizing a podcast is just one example of how you can diversify your income. You could also interview experts, transcribe the audio, edit the content, and use it in a guide, book, or online course.

Business risks need to be constantly evaluated, and over time, you'll likely become more risk-averse. The most dangerous number in business is one: one market, one service, one client, one boss, one invoice. Why risk everything on a single high-risk client or project, even if it seems like a sure thing?

Do you value your peace of mind? When you rely on just one source of income, you're at maximum risk. Yes, you need your first customer, but you should quickly strive to secure your second, third, and fourth clients. All you need to do is broaden your scope. If you managed to secure your first client, you can definitely secure more.

Scale

In my understanding, scale is about achieving a level of financial success that not only meets your needs but exceeds them. It's about increasing your sales in a systematic and efficient manner, leveraging assets and synergies for maximum impact.

Business, at its core, is about creating value. You don't necessarily have to be the one solving all the problems; knowing someone who can is often enough. Consider what other services or support your target market may need. Aim to grow your business by focusing on three main priorities, systematizing them, and then moving onto the next.

As you gain experience, identifying what your customers want or where they struggle becomes easier. With time, you'll become more adept at spotting opportunities.

When it comes to scaling, it's often more beneficial to be the one supplying tools to those striking out in new territories. For example, you might find more success helping bitcoin investors than investing in bitcoin yourself.

Every market has a top 20 percent of high-paying clients. Get to know these clients well, as they will become self-evident. Your business should have a sales filtering system to select the most suitable clients to work with.

Take the example of being an author: you write a book once, but it can be sold to thousands. Similarly, a website is coded once but can be visited by thousands. Among those visitors, some will find what they're looking for, and a subset of those may want more from you. This is where the 80:20 rule comes into play.

Ideally, clients should come to you. Outsourcing can help ensure your resources, time, and money are used efficiently. Consider book sales: Amazon promotes the books, collects the money, delivers the books, and pays you the remainder. This could potentially generate thousands a month, creating a passive income.

Passive incomes are desirable, and writing is a scalable way to achieve this. But don't limit yourself to just writing. Interviewing experts, for example, can provide valuable insights into your target market and generate content for a podcast or similar.

Strive to create content that can be repurposed in various ways, such as in ads, special reports, videos, articles, and online membership areas.

Writing is a crucial skill for making money. Before I wrote my first book, I knew technical authors and copywriters, but they never taught me how to write. I had to learn by reading and observing. Start by collecting items of interest for future reference. Remember, all writers start as avid readers.

Practicing writing through social media posts, emails, and replies can be beneficial. Writing a book is simply about writing in a structured manner on a topic you're passionate about. It's a peaceful, low-stress activity that doesn't cost much.

Planning a book is as simple as writing out bullet points on a familiar subject. The book will almost write itself, growing and evolving during the editing process. Think of a book as an extended PowerPoint proposal, with each bullet point a seed that can grow as fast as your enthusiasm allows.

This proposal aims to provide insights on how to establish a business without any initial capital, a method I used to start all my businesses. People are naturally curious about this topic, and sharing my experiences has led to the discovery of this book. Some readers may want to collaborate with you, purchase more of your books, or refer you or your books to others. It's a mutually beneficial process where everyone comes out a winner.

Even if the book doesn't generate sales or attract new clients, it's not a big deal. If the book doesn't perform well, it will go unnoticed, sparing you any embarrassment. However, if the book is well-received, that's a bonus.

Some readers will benefit more from your book than others. Those who are interested can find additional information on the book's accompanying website. This method is beneficial as it avoids aggressive sales strategies and allows you to assist readers, potentially sparking interest from those seeking further guidance.

It's unrealistic to expect to satisfy everyone all the time (just ask any politician, some of whom are admittedly delusional). Some people may not appreciate your transparency, while others may find your ideas too basic. However, if you genuinely strive to assist your readers, you're likely to succeed.

There are numerous ways you can contribute. You can write a book, create a PowerPoint presentation, host a webinar or a podcast, establish a membership website, distribute free software, or document business procedures. The creation of assets is highly scalable, and most assets can be digitally packaged, which can help your business grow exponentially.

Remember, you don't have to rely solely on your imagination or research to create assets. Documenting systematic business procedures is another way to generate an asset. This type of asset can be used in your own business or potentially sold under license to others, either as a blueprint for others to follow or as an outsourced service provided by your team.

At this point, many readers may feel a connection based on their current situation. Others may feel lost, as if we're communicating in a foreign language from an unknown location. The content may seem overly complex. The author is clearly a man, while the reader is a woman, and so on. It's easier for most people to find reasons not to act rather than to take action. We often focus on our differences rather than our similarities.

A more productive approach is to view objections as challenges and strive to adapt to your environment. This mindset can help you achieve more in life.

If you're feeling overwhelmed, revisit the ideas presented. Select the ones that resonate with you the most and prioritize them. Focus on the top three items, complete them, and then reprioritize. It's unrealistic to try to do everything at once, but it's entirely feasible to tackle a few ideas at a time.

Some may argue that these suggestions wouldn't work in their market. However, taking an idea from one industry and applying it to another where it hasn't been used before is a common strategy used by millionaires. This is the core of innovation. Numerous references highlight the importance of innovation in business. Your future success doesn't depend on what you have or what you value, but on how you utilize what you discover to benefit your customers.

Sales

Achieving success in business is largely dependent on our ability to sell and attract new customers. As entrepreneurs, selling is an essential skill. Despite the negative stereotypes often associated with salespeople, the art of selling is about facilitating the buying process for customers.

Think back to your childhood when you persuaded your parents to buy you an ice cream on a hot day. That's selling. From making a good first impression to delivering a persuasive presentation, we all engage in selling in some form.

The sales process can be as straightforward as engaging in friendly conversation with potential customers. Being overly persuasive isn't always beneficial. Sometimes, the most effective sales strategy is to simply guide people on what to do. For example, advising someone not to start a business until they've read a particular book. If you're interested in honing your persuasive skills, consider reading Robert Cialdini's book, Persuasion.

In my opinion, Neuro-Linguistic Programming (NLP) is a more practical tool. Although the author's explanation of how NLP works can be confusing, the techniques are natural and not overly manipulative. However, like everything else, moderation is key. Being too pushy in sales can be counterproductive.

If your product or service is exceptional, there's less need for hard sell tactics. High-pressure sales techniques can often deter potential customers. Encouraging customers to make a purchase should be a natural process. For me, the urgency to sell is often due to limited time availability. Timing is crucial in sales.

Remember, the most effective strategy is to attract customers to you. When customers approach you, they're more likely to be interested in what you're offering. They might admire your business, have heard good things about you, or need something you provide. In such cases, there's no need for aggressive sales tactics. In fact, the more pushy you are, the more likely you'll lose potential sales. When customers come to you, it's a clear indication that the timing is right.

The ultimate sales technique

We're masters in our field, but we often see the same avoidable errors happening over and over again. Many significant problems could be prevented if we simply communicated our message more effectively. Fortunately, there's a straightforward strategy that can help reduce these issues in the future. The key is to make it clear that you have a solution to a problem and are willing to offer a free initial consultation.

Offering a free consultation is a win-win situation. Sometimes, we can identify a simple solution right away, which is great for public relations and can lead to more referrals. Other times, we may need to provide a more comprehensive plan, which can help solve a major problem through our services.

Every professional, whether a doctor, lawyer, or insurance broker, offers a free consultation.

Why should you offer an initial free consultation?

During the first meeting, the professional typically assesses your needs free of charge. You come to them knowing you have a problem that needs fixing, and they provide further insights. These insights can help determine whether the issue requires serious intervention or if it will resolve itself naturally.

Consultations are generally a positive experience, providing relief and often leading to the discovery of new ways to manage the problem or lessen its impact. The goal is to minimize any potential negative effects and to define a clear path forward.

Every situation is unique. Personalized one-on-one consultations allow for clear communication focused on the main areas of concern. The consultation should help both parties understand whether the issue falls within the consultant's area of expertise.

If it doesn't, the consultant will typically refer you to someone who specializes in that area. However, these types of referrals are rare and usually only happen in highly technical cases. Most of the time, the consultant has the necessary expertise to discuss potential solutions.

Personalization is crucial

If you're examining this from a standpoint of offering advice, such as in the fields of health or cybersecurity, your aim is to have your advice heard and implemented by the recipient. The approach involves identifying the goal and then discussing the most effective ways to achieve it while maintaining robust health or cybersecurity measures. From a sales viewpoint, understanding the needs and objectives allows you to provide a solution that meets the core requirements and results in a successful sale. In both scenarios, satisfaction can be achieved by all parties involved, and this is how advice is not only heard but also acted upon. In many cases, a more comprehensive analysis of the facts may be conducted to ensure all aspects are thoroughly examined, increasing the likelihood of the proposed solution being effective. This is often followed by a proposal or a detailed prescription. The terminology can be used interchangeably. Additional questions may arise, and the solution may be adjusted to accommodate them. Some solutions may be automated, while others may require manual intervention. This is as true in the health sector as it is in business applications.

Avoid the forced imperative

Compulsory services are often unwelcome and seldom implemented. The consultative approach is particularly effective in situations where services are mandated. If you bypass the consultation process, you're likely to encounter more issues and incur higher costs. Everyone is given the same take-it-or-leave-it solution, resulting in decreased acceptance. Ensuring compliance becomes challenging, especially when the only options are coercion or failure. In the business world, clients have the option to switch providers, and they often do so without hesitation.

A good bedside manner instills good feelings

A good doctor, for instance, is often praised for their good bedside manner, which doesn't necessarily reflect their technical skills.

However, it significantly impacts the outcomes and trust patients place in them. The perception of better treatment may be an illusion, but the costs of service are likely to be lower, and overall patient (or client) satisfaction will be higher. The key difference lies in personalized consultation. This is why some restaurants are perceived as superior, even when the food is the same. The distinguishing factor is the personalized attention provided by the waiter.

The Waiter's Perspective

Looking at the role of a waiter from the perspective of giving advice and seeing that advice put into action, it becomes clear why this can be a beneficial role for a business, even if the waiter isn't involved in food preparation. The waiter, as the face of the business, typically welcomes new guests at the door, impeccably dressed, and immediately engages them with a question. This could be an offer of assistance, a query about what they're looking for, or an offer to guide them to a table. Regardless of the question, it's a natural conversation starter and is easily answered, allowing the waiter to immediately fulfill the guest's request, such as guiding them to a table. The waiter then continues to inquire about the guest's needs and preferences, potentially arranging the table and initial drinks, perhaps even something as simple as providing a water carafe. This is a full consultation process where the waiter is catering to the guest's needs, determining how they can assist, and then doing so. Guests will soon feel comfortable ordering food, likely appreciating suggestions from the knowledgeable waiter who can make recommendations that both ensure the guest's comfort and optimize the restaurant's kitchen operations, resulting in satisfied guests and a profitable business with potential for repeat customers.

The Advantage of a No-Pressure Approach

There's no need to pressure anyone into making a purchase at any point. Guests come seeking service and if it's provided satisfactorily, they stay. If the service is lacking or if they're drawn to another venue, they leave. If guests choose to stay and accept the offered service, it's because it made complete sense to them and felt right.

The Value of a Quality Consultation

There's no aggressive selling or obligation to buy, as simply providing service creates a win-win situation. Offering genuine, empathetic help is a great way to build goodwill, and as a result, more people will trust your advice. More people will recommend you as an expert in your field. If you're lucky, the consultation experience could lead to the creation of a positive reputation, with people sharing their experiences of working with you. This is the kind of narrative you want to be associated with. This is why this is the ultimate guide to ensuring potential customers come to you, listen to your advice, and act on it.

Next up: What to Sell and When to Sell It: Expect to go through tough times before you experience success. Don't succumb to unforeseen pressures; serving customers will require some adjustments. You'll get to identify your start-up type, which will provide insights into how to position your business and what to look for in potential customers. The next chapter will guide you away from potential disasters. This is exactly why you need to be aware of potential pitfalls and have strategies to avoid them.

Conclusion

We've determined that the primary objective should be to gain a customer. We've discussed the significant advantages a customer brings to your business. We've shown how having a customer is essential for defining your venture as a business rather than a hobby. This knowledge alone is often sufficient for those in the early stages of a start-up, but there's more to it.

The need for a customer isn't typically the first thing that comes to mind for budding entrepreneurs. We tend to become engrossed in the details of establishing and preparing to launch a business, or in the appealing technology or necessary skills. These are all exciting aspects, but customers are primarily interested in results.

Many start-ups make the mistake of chasing an idealized vision. Customers, however, accurately represent the specific group of people who can assist you in turning your vision into reality. Therefore, the sooner you acquire a customer, the sooner you can validate whether your vision is something they're willing to pay for. You might find that you need to adjust your strategy to make your vision a reality, and most of us value such feedback.

It's universally agreed upon that we never seem to have enough time or money. We all desire more. Interestingly, focusing on a customer can also lead to more money. When we concentrate on a customer, we tend to ignore other things, most of which are distractions. A customer is the key to fulfilling your needs and much more.

As your start-up grows and attracts more customers, your customer goals will likely change. Initially, you're a unique unknown entity, but over time, your business will become reliable and stable. As a start-up entrepreneur, you should be prepared for these changes.

It's important to spend time building the habit of creating assets, with customers being assets themselves. These assets can be leveraged to develop your intellectual property and market position. The consistent development of assets will ultimately help you show why you're the best choice for your customers. Wherever possible, assets should be shareable and capable of going viral to generate buzz and excitement in the market.

You will need to change and adapt

Initially, you might cater to a specific type of customer that is easy to please. This approach can generate immediate cash flow and buy you the time you need. Ideally, you'll be able to satisfy a sufficient number of customers to finance the next phase of your business. This success can then enable you to shift your focus to customers who align more closely with your long-term business vision. Remember, the journey to success isn't always a straight line.

As you begin to acquire your first customers, it's essential to work closely with them to ensure you can meet their needs effectively.

It's always a good idea to exceed their expectations to keep them fully satisfied. You may start collecting testimonials or developing the capability to create use cases, or, with their consent, publish customer-approved testimonials and case studies.

As your business evolves, you'll discover new market opportunities. You'll also need to establish consistent, cost-effective sales systems and processes to attract new customers. Simultaneously, you'll learn to recognize your premium customers and develop a scalable strategy to convert customers into clients.

Growing your business will inevitably put pressure on other aspects, including the need to increase overheads and improve cash flow. You'll find more effective ways to finance sales based on your understanding of client behavior. It's crucial to manage these issues carefully as your business transitions from startup to a more established entity.

Over time, you'll find creative ways to market your stories and assets. You'll become more proficient at exceeding customer expectations and gain a better understanding of your target audience. You'll also identify the markets where you fit best and understand why customers choose you. This knowledge will make it easier for you to increase sales and grow your business.

You'll gradually build a reputation in your market, possibly in an emerging market or a new niche within an existing market. You'll gain a better understanding of your market position and find ways to enhance it. Your focus will eventually narrow down to a group of potential customers who are abundant and willing to do business with you. They, in turn, will find it easy to view you in a positive light.

Competence, confidence, and capability

As time goes on, your business should continue to expand. The more you tailor your offerings to your customers, the more likely you'll be able to turn them into clients. You'll begin to secure long-term contracts, with some clients placing ongoing or rolling orders. As your business matures, you may find that banks start to view you favorably. They might even offer financial services to support your customer and client needs, significantly aiding your growth.

In the early stages, don't expect too much financial assistance. However, help usually becomes available as you start to secure initial clients and repeat business.

If you've made it this far, you deserve a hearty congratulations. Many people never receive the acknowledgment they deserve for their hard work. Most people simply assume that you're doing what you're supposed to do, and after all, you're making money from it, right?

So, allow me to commend you on your success. I understand how challenging it can be, even though it might sound easy.

Printed in Great Britain
by Amazon

54059571R00076